STUDIES IN ECONOMIC AND SOCIAL HISTORY

This series, specially commissioned by the Economic History Society, provides a guide to the current interpretations of the key themes of economic and social history in which advances have recently been made or in which there has been significant debate.

Originally entitled 'Studies in Economic History', in 1974 the series had its scope extended to include topics in social history, and the new series title, 'Studies in Economic and Social History', signalises this development.

The series gives readers access to the best work done, helps them to draw their own conclusions in major fields of study, and by means of the critical bibliography in each book guides them in the selection of further reading. The aim is to provide a springboard to further work rather than a set of pre-packaged conclusions or short-cuts.

ECONOMIC HISTORY SOCIETY

The Economic History Society, which numbers over 3000 members, publishes the *Economic History Review* four times a year (free to members) and holds an annual conference. Enquiries about membership should be addressed to the Assistant Secretary, Economic History Society, Peterhouse, Cambridge. Full-time students may join the Society at special rates.

D1078485

00087100

STUDIES IN ECONOMIC AND SOCIAL HISTORY

Edited for the Economic History Society by M. W. Flinn

PUBLISHED

B. W. E. Alford Depression and Recovery? British Economic Growth, 1918–1939
S. D. Chapman The Cotton Industry in the Industrial Revolution
R. A. Church The Great Victorian Boom, 1850–1873
D. C. Coleman Industry in Tudor and Stuart England
P. L. Cottrell British Overseas Investment in the Nineteenth Century
Ralph Davis English Overseas Trade, 1500–1700
M. E. Falkus The Industrialisation of Russia, 1700–1914
M. W. Flinn British Population Growth, 1700–1850
J. R. Hay The Origins of the Liberal Welfare Reforms, 1906–1914
R. H. Hilton The Decline of Serfdom in Medieval England
E. L. Jones The Development of English Agriculture, 1815–1873
J. D. Marshall The Old Poor Law, 1795–1834
Alan S. Milward The Economic Effects of the Two World Wars on Britain
G. E. Mingay Enclosure and the Small Farmer in the Age of the Industrial Revolution
A. E. Musson British Trade Unions, 1800–1875
R. B. Outhwaite Inflation in Tudor and Early Stuart England
P. L. Payne British Entrepreneurship in the Nineteenth Century
Michael E. Rose The Relief of Poverty, 1834–1914
S. B. Saul The Myth of the Great Depression, 1873–1896
Arthur J. Taylor Laissez-faire and State Intervention in Nineteenth-century Britain
Peter Temin Causal Factors in American Economic Growth in the Nineteenth Century

TITLES IN PREPARATION INCLUDE

F. Caron and *G. Holmes* The Performance of the French Economy, 1870–1939
J. R. Chartres Internal Trade in England in the Sixteenth and Seventeenth Centuries
Richard Johnson Education and Society, 1780–1870
J. H. S. Kent Religion and Society in England in the Nineteenth Century
J.Lovell British Trade Unions, 1875–1933
R. M. Mitchison British Population Growth, 1850–1950
R. J. Morris Class and Social Structure in the Industrial Revolution
G. D. Ramsay The Woollen Cloth Industry, 1500–1750
S. B. Saul The New Deal
Joan Thirsk The Changing Regional Structure of English Agriculture in the Sixteenth and Seventeenth Centuries

The Great Victorian Boom
1850–1873

Prepared for
the Economic History Society by

R. A. CHURCH

Professor of Economic History,
University of East Anglia

© The Economic History Society 1975

All rights reserved. No part of this publication
may be reproduced or transmitted, in any form
or by any means, without permission.

First published 1975 by
THE MACMILLAN PRESS LTD
London and Basingstoke
Associated companies in New York Dublin
Melbourne Johannesburg and Madras

SBN 333 14350 7

Printed in Great Britain by
THE ANCHOR PRESS LTD
Tiptree, Essex

BATH COLLEGE OF
HIGHER EDUCATION
NEWTON PARK LIBRARY

CLASS No.
330.942081 CHU

SUPPLIER
Don

This book is sold subject to the standard
conditions of the Net Book Agreement.

The paperback edition of this book is sold subject to the condition
that it shall not, by way of trade or otherwise, be lent, resold,
hired out, or otherwise circulated without the publisher's prior
consent in any form of binding or cover other than that in which
it is published and without a similar condition including this condition being imposed on the subsequent purchaser.

Contents

Acknowledgements

I wish to record my gratitude to A. W. Coats, P. L. Cottrell, T. R. Gourvish, R. J. Irving, W. M. Mathew and S. B. Saul, each of whom read all or part of the manuscript and offered valuable suggestions. The remaining imperfections, whether in exposition or interpretation, are not in any way the responsibility of those whose advice I took or chose to disregard.

R. A. C.

Note on References

References in the text within square brackets relate to the numbered items in the Select Bibliography, followed, where necessary, by the page number in italics, for example [131: *217*]. Other references in the text, numbered consecutively throughout the book, relate to annotations of the text or to sources not given in the Select Bibliography, and are itemised in the Notes and References section.

Editor's Preface

SO long as the study of economic and social history was confined to a small group at a few universities, its literature was not prolific and its few specialists had no great problem in keeping abreast of the work of their colleagues. Even in the 1930s there were only two journals devoted exclusively to economic history and none at all to social history. But the high quality of the work of the economic historians during the inter-war period and the post-war growth in the study of the social sciences sparked off an immense expansion in the study of economic history after the Second World War. There was a great expansion of research and many new journals were launched, some specialising in branches of the subject like transport, business or agricultural history. Most significantly, economic history began to be studied as an aspect of history in its own right in schools. As a consequence, the examining boards began to offer papers in economic history at all levels, while textbooks specifically designed for the school market began to be published. As a specialised discipline, social history is an even more recent arrival in the academic curriculum. Like economic history, it, too, is rapidly generating a range of specialist publications. The importance of much of the recent work in this field and its close relationship with economic history have therefore prompted the Economic History Society to extend the scope of this series – formerly confined to economic history – to embrace themes in social history.

For those engaged in research and writing this period of rapid expansion of studies has been an exciting, if rather breathless one. For the larger numbers, however, labouring in the outfield of the schools and colleges of further education, the excitement of the explosion of research has been tempered by frustration arising from its vast quantity and, frequently, its controversial character. Nor, it must be admitted, has the ability or willing-

7

ness of the academic historians to generalise and summarise marched in step with their enthusiasm for research.

The greatest problems of interpretation and generalisation have tended to gather round a handful of principal themes in economic and social history. It is, indeed, a tribute to the sound sense of economic and social historians that they have continued to dedicate their energies, however inconclusively, to the solution of these key problems. The results of this activity, however, much of it stored away in a wide range of academic journals, have tended to remain inaccessible to many of those currently interested in the subject. Recognising the need for guidance through the burgeoning and confusing literature that has grown around these basic topics, the Economic History Society hopes in this series of short books to offer some help to students and teachers. The books are intended to serve as guides to current interpretations in major fields of economic and social history in which important advances have recently been made, or in which there has recently been some significant debate. Each book aims to survey recent work, to indicate the full scope of the particular problem as it has been opened up by recent scholarship, and to draw such conclusions as seem warranted, given the present state of knowledge and understanding. The authors will often be at pains to point out where, in their view, because of a lack of information or inadequate research, they believe it is premature to attempt to draw firm conclusions. While authors will not hesitate to review recent and older work critically, the books are not intended to serve as vehicles for their own specialist views: the aim is to provide a balanced summary rather than an exposition of the author's own viewpoint. Each book will include a descriptive bibliography.

In this way the series aims to give all those interested in economic and social history at a serious level access to recent scholarship in some major fields. Above all, the aim is to help the reader to draw his own conclusions, and to guide him in the selection of further reading as a means to this end, rather than to present him with a set of pre-packaged conclusions.

M. W. FLINN

University of Edinburgh   *Editor*

1 Introduction

THE coinage of a memorable phrase or seductive epithet to describe this or that phenomenon is a common device for drawing popular attention to it. Thus, the 'Great Depression' was derived from the *Royal Commission on the Depression of Trade and Industry* in 1886, which offered an opportunity for merchants and manufacturers to ventilate their concern over foreign competition. Subsequently the period to which the 'Great Depression' applied was extended by historians to cover the years between 1873 and 1896, when falling prices appeared to be the dominant trend. This revisionism, one of the imperatives of historical research, is an important part of the historiographical process, for in attempting to describe and explain the past the historian necessarily resorts to compression and comparison in order to highlight the major contrasts and similarities in historical trends, problems and periods. Such a process requires categorisation and labelling as a legitimate shorthand device for isolating what is peculiar or particularly significant. Unfortunately there is a danger not only that historians' labels may distract us from the complexity of historical change but also that they will persist after research findings have undermined their validity. Labels conceived by contemporaries cannot be lightly dismissed even if with handsight they seem to have been inaccurate, and despite Saul's powerful assault upon *The Myth of the Great Depression, 1873–1896* (1969), it can be argued that the phrase continues to be valid inasmuch as this represents the mainstream interpretation by contemporaries of their own experience, and therefore is of interest in its own right. The 'Great Victorian Boom' can claim no such historical pedigree, for it is one of several phrases commonly used by historians since that time to convey the distinctive character of the mid-nineteenth century, 'when the economic troubles of the preceding generation seemed to vanish as if by magic' [131:*217*]. As the 1840s receded and the gold discoveries in California (1848) and Australia (1851) began to take effect, we are told, it was a 'new era of prosperity that now dawned' [4:*163*].

Spliced chronologically between the excitement of the debate on the origins of Industrial Revolution and that on the difficulties and dilemmas posed by foreign competition and the so-called Great Depression, the relatively successful mid-Victorian decades have suffered neglect. Assumptions have too often been substituted for research, while the complexities of the period remain largely unexplored. None the less, the 'good', or 'golden years', as the period was commonly described in the textbooks forty years ago, still reappear, though these have also been transformed, almost imperceptibly, into mid-Victorian prosperity, mid-Victorian boom and – the ultimate hyperbole – the Great Victorian Boom. This shift in perspective is partly explicable in terms of the influence of the ideas and research of Kondratief, Schumpeter and Kuznets. Building upon Kondratief's conceptualisation of the dynamics of economic activity as occurring in a series of trends, each of about fifty years' duration, Schumpeter and Kuznets identified a series of lesser, alternating long swings in production (sometimes known as Kuznets cycles), the price movements associated with them forming the main criteria for the periodisation and characterisation of economic activity [140:*chs vi,vii*; 99:*ch.iv*].

For the British economy the much-quoted work of Layton and Crowther, containing chapters called 'Prices Falling 1822–1849', 'Prices Rising 1849–1874' and 'Prices Falling 1874–1914', seems to have encouraged such an interpretation, despite the qualifications which appear in their text [19:*67*]. These were the chronological divisions which in Rostow's seminal study underpinned the analysis of economic trends, and despite his own reservations about the ambiguity in describing the period 1847 to 1873 as the great mid-Victorian boom [23:*9,20*], since then others, whose texts are more widely known, have shown less caution. Thus, Checkland alluded to the general economic expansion accompanied from 1853 by a trend of rising prices 'which mounted all the way to 1873' [5:*27*], whereas Hobsbawm referred to 'the upswing of the "golden

years" of the Victorians' from the late 1840s to 1873 [81:296].
Checkland mentioned entrepreneurial exhilaration as a feature of the 1850s and 1860s which he contrasts with the 'long struggle against falling prices' of preceding decades [5:27]. This is equivalent to the 'business malaise' of those years which Hobsbawm identified as one of the contrasting characteristics which distinguished the 'twenty-five years of inflation' (1848–73) from the 'price fluctuation or deflation' of previous decades, and indeed from the period which followed [81:296]. E. V. Morgan located the great boom between 1858 and 1873 [114:161,187], but Kindleberger, detecting an earlier starting-point in 1850, was unsure of the terminal date, 1873 or 1875 marking the end of a period of 'unified or very rapid growth' [95:10]. The most recent and unequivocal reaffirmation of the conventional orthodoxy comes from Best, who contrasted 'the euphoria of the boom decades of the 1850s and 1860s with the gloom of the so-called "great depression" ' [3:1]. He maintained that the economic trends of this period provided the least disputable ground for regarding the years between 1850 and 1873 as possessing a unity.

From our standpoint of long-term trends we choose to disregard as unimportant the discrepancies in dating this somewhat ill-defined phenomenon of unity, but the notion that such a unity existed merits careful consideration. Necessarily this requires a reappraisal of the Great mid-Victorian Boom and a re-examination of the typical elements which historians have associated with it, conferring upon the third quarter of the century, or thereabouts, a distinctiveness in contrast with similar time periods either side: rising prices and wages; expanding investment, production and trade; increasing prosperity; and a generally optimistic climate of opinion, especially among the business community. To the extent that we can identify these features in our period we shall also seek to explain them.

It is important to emphasise at the outset that much of the statistical evidence available for our period is often less than completely reliable, while estimates derived from it are frequently dubious and are employed here only in the absence of more dependable qualitative material. Even though we shall

11

pay more attention to the direction in which various statistical series move and to their relation to movements in other series rather than to their absolute levels, we acknowledge the pitfalls and try not to impose more weight upon the statistical data than they will bear.

2 Prices and Economic Growth

(i) PRICE TRENDS

I T is difficult to understand the origins of the notion that the period between 1850 and 1873 was one of generally rising prices. Two leading contemporary economists and statisticians, Robert Giffen and W. S. Jevons, stressed the discontinuity in trend produced by the sharp price rise between 1853 and 1857. Both viewed the period from 1850 to 1873 as one of price stability, or possibly mild inflation [73: 77–91; 87: 146]. Why, then, has it since become customary to describe these years as a time of rising prices? Like contemporaries we are dependent in our discussion of price trends upon wholesale price data relating mainly to leading articles, raw materials and provisions. The exclusion of retail prices from the analysis is unfortunate, because the number and value of transactions in articles after they leave the manufacturers' hands and on their way to the consumer probably exceeds the number and value of similar transactions in the raw-material stage. The prices of manufactured articles are almost wholly excluded from the overall price indices available for the period, and as the tendency within industry in our period was towards the diminution in the real costs of manufacturing and distribution, their exclusion from the price index, admittedly due to the paucity of data, distorts the weighting of the index in favour of more volatile wholesale commodity prices. The effect is to exaggerate the degree of price inflation. Furthermore, an average price index can also be deceptive because of the changes in individual prices which it conceals. Thus, while fibrous materials – cotton, wool and flax – and animal products rose in price in the 1850s, 1860s and early 1870s, the prices of tin, copper, hides, tea, sugar, coffee, oats and barley rose in the 1850s but merely maintained the higher levels in the 1860s. It is striking, however, that whereas most raw-material prices moved upwards for all or much of the period (coal is an important exception) the prices of semi-manufactured goods, yarns and cloths for example, were less volatile, and this applied even more to manufactured goods. Pig- and bar-iron prices actually fell, as did some glass prices [88: *passim*]. Table 1 (p. 15) indicates the variations in selected price indices.

The picture is thus a complex one, but while the relatively stable trend in average prices from 1854 to 1870 in fact conceals marked and unsynchronised fluctuations of individual commodities, the substantial price inflation of the early 1850s stands out in all the *general* price indices available, and thus qualifies as an historical fact which merits investigation. It was this initial spurt in wholesale prices, whose origins they identified in 1849, to which Layton and Crowther drew attention in a chapter misleadingly entitled 'Prices Rising 1849–1874', but they noted that thereafter prices remained stationary for a decade and a half, while a second, equally short though smaller, rise carried the index to a new peak in 1873 [19: *73*]. This profile of stability is concealed in the Rousseaux index due to the weighting of cotton textiles, for the cotton famine, caused by the American Civil War in 1861–4, brought extraordinarily high prices which have the effect of pushing the overall level upward. It seems, however, that Layton and Crowther's titles proved more memorable than the chapters themselves, for the qualifications they made were largely ignored, and for more than twenty years the third quarter of the century was portrayed, by Rostow and other historians, as a period of secular price inflation. Such a view continues to appear in the textbooks, despite the reassertion, notably by Saville [24: *67*] and Landes [18: *233*], of interpretations similar to those advanced by contemporary economists. Indeed, Landes maintained that a very long-term perspective of protracted deflation from 1817 to 1897 threw into relief a price plateau in the mid-Victorian period, when the boom of the early 1850s brought only six or seven years of rising prices. In fact, the Rousseaux price index, which was his source, shows that very rapid acceleration occurred in 1853 and 1854 and that the experience of acute

14

Table 1

Selected Price Indices: 1847–50 = 100*

	Upland or Middling American (raw cotton)	Cotton Yarn	Piece Goods (plain)	Piece Goods (printed)	Stockings and Socks	Flax	Linen Yarn	Linen Manufactures (plain)
1847–50	100	100	100	100	100	100	100	100
1851–5	99	97	93	96	88	118	110	106
1856–60	122	103	96	94	74	108	123	103
1861–5	342	191	145	121	88	125	140	108
1866–70	211	185	130	117	92	121	147	107
1871–5	156	152	107	109	88	110	142	108

	Lincoln Half Hog (raw wool)	Woollen and Worsted Yarn	Woollen Cloths	Flannels	Stuffs	Carpets
1847–50	100	100	100	100	100	100
1851–5	128	102	86	95	82	96
1856–60	165	123	91	103	88	96
1861–5	210	153	115	128	107	99
1866–70	159	156	128	121	118	114
1871–5	204	157	135	122	104	117

	Hides (river plates, dry)	Leather (crop 30–40 lb.)	Pig Iron (scots)	Iron Bars (common)	Coal (London market)	Coal (export)	Glass (common bottles)
1847–50	100	100	100	100	100	100	100
1851–5	135	120	122	111	110	139	93
1856–60	207	167	123	104	103	121	93
1861–5	169	147	111	98	105	119	86
1866–70	152	147	113	95	104	129	86
1871–5	201	175	177	135	138	199	88

SOURCES: Prices of British goods delivered at Hamburg collated by A. Soetbeer, in *Royal Commission on Precious Metals, Accounts and Papers*, XIV, C. 5512–1 (1888), app. xvi, pp. 236–7. The indices for raw cotton, wool flax, hides, pig iron, bar iron and coals are based on prices quoted by A. Sauerbeck, 'Prices of Commodities and the Precious Metals', *Journal of the Statistical Society*, XLIX (1886).

* The Rousseaux overall price index for 1847–50 is 101, which suggests that this is a reasonable base period adopted by Soetbeer.

inflation was even briefer than Landes inferred (see Figure 1). The price rise in 1856–7 was only 3 per cent [112:*472*]. Clearly the relationships between the booms of the 1850s and 1870s are of critical importance in influencing the way one approaches the mid-Victorian economy, whose distinctive characteristic, it now appears, was that of high but – making allowance for cotton-famine prices – relatively stable prices, intervening between the period of spectacular but short-lived price inflations of 1853 to 1855 and 1870 to 1873. We need to explain the sudden steep ascent to the price plateau of the mid-1850s and 1860s, and the continuance of relatively high price trends until after the American Civil War.

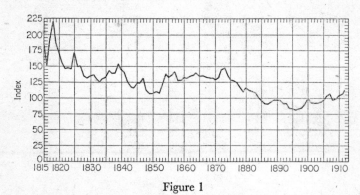

Figure 1

Wholesale Prices in Britain, 1815–1913 (1900 = 100)

SOURCE: S. B. Saul, *The Myth of the Great Depression, 1873-1896* (1969).

(ii) MONETARY FACTORS

Contemporary economists and statisticians were convinced that they knew why prices had risen. Indeed, even as news of the gold discoveries in California in 1848 and in Australia in 1852 were announced, confident predictions were made by economists, notably Cairnes and Jevons, arguing from the quantity theory of money, that price levels would increase in a proportion which the new gold bore to the total gold in circulation [137: *575–601*]. Some other contemporaries stressed other aspects of the gold discoveries, and William Newmarch, economist and

16

statistician, laid emphasis on the expansion of what he called 'effective demand' for the output of goods and services for the whole world and the effect of investment in the gold fields [122:7]. However, the monetary interpretation of price inflation, expressed by Cairnes, Jevons and Giffen, became the conventional view [80], and continued to dominate discussions on the problem for a very long time. The interpretation rested upon the quantity theory of money in a simple form, in which the level of prices and the level of production were directly determined by the money supply (strictly defined as notes and coin held by the public, and bank deposits, but which may also, as in our discussion, include quasi-money, mainly in the form of bills of exchange or finance bills).

Abstracting from the effects of new gold on income and employment, the purely monetary effects of gold would be to raise the money supply and induce a rise in the prices of goods and services. Even assuming that there was no change in the attitudes of individuals to holding liquid assets, and that the speed with which money changed hands remained unaltered, the value of transactions would increase, until people's demand for money, and their unwillingness to hold it, was at a level corresponding with the increased stock of money at this new and higher level of prices. Walters's recent work on the money supply in the United Kingdom since 1880 led him to conclude that its effect on prices and income was significant and that it was in the direction predicted by the quantity theory [154]. Differential movements, both of degree and chronology, in the prices of various commodities argue against acceptance of a solely monetarist explanation of price behaviour. None the less, theory and inference suggest that we should regard as a strong hypothesis the view which accords to money supply a causal role in the inflation of the 1850s and we shall proceed, therefore, to explore the particular mechanism behind this process.

Between 1848 and 1857 the aggregate addition to the commercial world's stock of gold was estimated by Newmarch to have been an unprecedented 30 per cent, an increase which, in terms of initial spending into the income stream by gold producers, was more than triple the rate between 1841 and 1850 and many times greater than earlier periods. Via trading mechanisms perhaps 60 per cent of all gold entering Europe came to Britain [19: 67–70], causing a rapid augmentation of the Bank of England's reserves. The Bank's response was to reduce interest rates and increase discounts, the effect of which was to swell the reserves of commercial bankers, thereby increasing lending potential. In this way cheap money helped to boost recovery which led to the boom of the early 1850s [12: 243]. If money supply was causally related to price movements, then, according to Rostow, assuming the marginal efficiency of capital to have remained unaltered we would have expected rapidly increasing gold supplies to have depressed interest rates and raised prices; and when the gold influx ceased, prices would have fallen and interest rates risen. But after the initial price inflation, even until the mid-1860s the overall price level *remained* high. Interest rates appear to have risen marginally, if unsteadily [13: 235], though estimates of real rates of interest, which take account of price changes, moved much more erratically with trend neither up nor down. Even so, neither nominal nor real rates exceeded 5 per cent often, and the levels generally ruled higher than they did in the 1870s and 1880s, when the British economy was alleged to have been affected by gold shortage. It was for this reason that Rostow rejected the importance of gold and the influence of monetary factors on the levels of prices and interest rates.

Several factors may provide a solution to the 'Rostow Paradox'.[1] First, it seems likely that the efficiency of capital did alter, as economic recovery from the depression of 1848 gathered momentum, assisted by the income effects of the gold discoveries themselves [12: 285]. Second, the boom of 1852–3 itself generated a bullion drain through the balance of payments, mainly to pay for food and raw materials; in defence of its reserves the Bank of England reduced note circulation, raised Bank Rate and curtailed discounting. The repetition of such a sequence may also help to explain the absence of any long-term fall in interest rates [13: 235]. Third, is the hypothetical, but plausible, possibility that the lagged response of bankers to new gold-based liquidity levels in the early 1850s was to shift to lower liquidity ratios, choosing to live dangerously. This would be consistent with the typically over-loaned position of the banks in the mid-nineteenth century [22:*57*], though demonstrable proof that such a change did occur is difficult to establish, because ratios varied widely, both in the short term and between banks [138:*178*].

The Landes view is that a virtually autonomous credit expansion, resulting from the growth of banks and banking services, on an international as well as national basis and to some extent independent of gold, largely explains why the inflated price levels generated initially in the early 1850s persisted for so long. The growth of the banking sector is undeniable, yet it is possible that offsetting this was the trend towards improved liquidity, clearly evident after 1870 but which may have begun already in our period, as the extension of limited liability and the publication of figures encouraged more conservative practice [153:*230–3*] following the pioneering stage of joint-stock banking in the 1830s and 1840s. The precise contribution of the banks in augmenting the money supply is problematical, but Hughes and Nishimura have shown that means of payment originating outside the banks, mainly in the form of bills of exchange, continued to expand [12, 22], circumventing the restrictions on money supply imposed by the Bank Charter Act of 1844.[2] The reason why the volume of commercial bills was positively correlated with interest rates down to the crisis of 1866 is that interest rates were less volatile than profit expectations, which in the periods of expanding production and trade exceeded the level of interest rates [22:*67–74*]. We may conclude tentatively from this that, although in the boom of the early 1850s gold and the Bank of England's cheap-money policy contributed initially to rising prices, thereafter the public's demand for money may have constituted the chief stimulus to the money supply.

The apparent buoyancy of interest rates in a period when the money supply was rising can be interpreted as an indication of an even more rapid extension of demand (for money) than supply. This would be congruent with the thesis advanced by R. H. Patterson in 1865 in *The New Golden Age*, that the growth in trade required enlarged gold supplies in order to enable countries to settle trading deficits, and that because of this the new gold was arguably a necessary, though not sufficient, condition for the secular economic expansion in the mid-nineteenth century. In the short term, the fact that prices and interest rates rose, and that net expansion of reserves provided a broader base than would have existed before 1848, meant that the booms in prices and production could develop further and over a longer period than would otherwise have been the case. The pressures on international liquidity derived in part from the appreciation of silver caused by the influx of new gold, and lasted for at least ten years. The resulting dislocation in the monetary order took the form in the 1850s of a drain of undervalued silver to Asia, where European countries were in deficit on balance of payments; competition for the new gold ensued, notably between the Bank of France and the Bank of England, each attempting to protect reserves [114: *177–8*]. This state of affairs persisted into the 1860s, when by stimulating a search for alternative raw-cotton supplies the American Civil War indirectly caused a further drain to the East. The re-discount policies of the quasi-central banks of Europe were instrumental in helping to ease the problems of international liquidity and short-term crisis, which, paradoxically, were features of the age of new gold.

(iii) NON-MONETARY FACTORS

The major influence on the current periodisation of the nineteenth century into long swings has been W. W. Rostow's *The British Economy of the 19th Century* [23], in which the purely monetary significance of gold was disregarded. He argued that the strictly monetary effects of the new gold, operating through central bank reserves of the Bank of England and interest rates, do not appear to have been important; that there was no evidence to suggest that the banking systems of the nineteenth century required as much gold as was mined in order to avoid the imposition of deflationary policies. Subsequent research has demonstrated that, notwithstanding increased world gold supplies, external drains of bullion were major elements in the upper turning-points of the business cycles between 1847 and 1873 adding further support to the view, expressed, for example, by William Newmarch [6:*366*], which attaches importance to the new gold in enlarging international liquidity at a time when it threatened to hamper trade expansion [43]. But Rostow argued that, even supposing the new gold was in fact required for the successful working of the bank systems of the world, mining would still constitute a tax, a drain on resources from alternative uses. It was in this respect, he argued, that, like a war, or the building of a pyramid, gold was a non-productive, price-raising factor, quite apart from any possible effect it might have had on central bank reserves, the rate of interest, and the willingness of banking systems to lend [23:*10–11*]. While with respect to gold-mining this effect may have contributed to price inflation during the years of fuller employment and rising prices 1852–5, nevertheless, if one excludes, as Rostow did, the effects of gold-mining on currency and banking, it seems unlikely that the price-raising effects were very important. It is the non-productive character of expenditure on war and gold-mining, in Rostow's model financed out of inflationary sources and new money, which causes price inflation; and whereas Sayers maintained the discoveries were followed by a growth of capital, he argued that this was only possible through forms of saving involving the re-allocation of expenditure between investment and consumption [138:*581*].

Since that time the Keynesian theory of employment and income has focused attention on the kind of approach adopted by Newmarch in the 1850s, for which Sayers showed little sympathy, and Hughes has analysed systematically the income effects of the gold discoveries which had hitherto been absent from much of the literature on gold and the economy. The discoveries generated incomes, first in connection with mining activities, and later secondary and tertiary demands were made upon industry and the sources of raw materials for industry. The demand for goods and services in the United States and Australia proceeded to increase, not only within the gold-producing areas, but within a short space of time affected manufacturers and merchants in Lancashire and Birmingham and their raw-material suppliers. In this way the new gold came to Britain as payment for British goods and services, stimulated investment and incomes, and precipitated a steep rise in prices of those commodities, notably textiles and leather goods, with high supply inelasticities [12:*16–17*]. This situation was accentuated by the military and naval demand for these items. Indeed, Rostow stressed the importance of war expenditure as another form of non-productive inflationary expenditure in this period. For the Crimean War, coming as it did in a period of close to full employment, was financed mainly by government borrowing, rather than taxation, and when the war was in full swing ran at almost the same level as the value of British exports. However, since the initial price inflation, which reached a peak in 1853–4, preceded the Crimean campaign commencing late in 1854, this factor can only have been important in sustaining the new high level of prices. The same can be said of the spectacular rise in the prices of textile fibres during the American Civil War.

On balance, the evidence we have reviewed here suggests that, during the cyclical recovery from the lower turning-point in 1848, monetary and income effects of the new gold provided added impetus, which carried wholesale prices to unprecedented peacetime heights. These levels cannot be ascribed to a unitary cause. High prices were maintained by a combination of rapid expansion in the demand for raw materials in inelastic supply (compounded in the 1860s by acute scarcity of fibres caused by the American Civil War); inflationary expenditure associated with the war in the Crimea, the United States, and Europe; a high level of demand and credit inflation.

(iv) PRICES AND PRODUCTION

The course of economic growth itself has been subject to disagreement among historians. For many years textbooks have presented the Great Victorian Boom as the economic *dénouement* of industrial revolution, but this interpretation is not that presented by Deane and Cole's path-breaking study of *British Economic Growth 1688–1959* [56] and it is that which has been incorporated in other recent and important studies [119, 126]. Before Deane and Cole, Walter Hoffman's well-known index of industrial production, despite its deficiencies, had been accepted as the best indicator available for the study of economic development in the nineteenth century,[3] and this showed the most rapid rates of growth occurring in the years between the end of the Napoleonic Wars and the 1850s, the annual rate of growth of industrial production falling from above 3 per cent for the decades before 1855 to below 3 per cent between 1856 and 1876 [82:*31*]. The index thus suggested a falling off in the rate of growth in the mid-century although, of course, the absolute increments to output were very large. Hoffman's index was derived from diverse sources of information on inputs of raw materials and the physical output of commodities; Deane and Cole's estimates were derived from equally miscellaneous income estimates to which price deflators were applied [56:*283*]. The result was an index of industrial output which showed not merely a deceleration in the mid-century rate of growth, in accord with Hoffman's findings, but an actual dip, followed by a considerable revival before the end of the century. The course of gross national product showed the same, and the slower mid-century rate of growth, which was even more marked in the *per capita* figures, suggested to Deane and Cole a lower rate of growth in productivity at this stage. The weakness of this approach is that the Rousseaux price index used in the deflation process is an index of raw materials, rather than manufactured goods, and would produce accurate results only if there were no considerable changes in the relation between raw material prices and manufacturing prices in this period.

We know, however, that this was not the case (p. 14). In the later nineteenth century raw-material prices were falling much faster than the prices of manufactures, the effect of which on the Deane and Cole index was to overstate growth for that period [162:*406*]. Taking account of this criticism Phyllis Deane has recently constructed revised estimates based on expenditure data [8:*97*], which show the long-term peak rates of expansion occurring between the 1840s and 1870s when G.N.P. for the United Kingdom grew at less than 2·5 per cent per annum and average G.N.P. at less than 2 per cent. The longest period of sustained expansion seems to have been in the seventeen-year period between 1858 and 1875 when G.N.P. is estimated to have grown at about 2·8 per cent per annum compound, and 2 per cent per head of population (see Table

2). While the rate of growth is relatively low in comparison with growth rates in other countries at a similar phase of industrialisation,[4] nevertheless the revised estimates do fit the conventional interpretation of the later part of this period, at least, as one of considerable economic expansion. The precise relationships between prices and growth are obscure, for if Deane's new figures are correct, the maximum secular growth rate appears to have *followed* the rapid inflation of the early 1850s, in a period of relatively stable, then marginally falling, prices, interrupted by the inflationary boom of 1870–3. We also need to warn against exaggerating the contrast which Ashworth,

Table 2

Long-term Rates of Growth in United Kingdom Gross National Product: Annual Percentage Rates of Compound Growth Calculated as Between Averages for Decades

	Total G.N.P.	Average G.N.P.
1830/9–1860/9	1·97	1·61
1835/44–1865/74	2·36	1·85
1840/9–1870/9	2·42	1·85
1845/54–1875/84	2·31	1·59
1850/9–1880/9	2·15	1·46
1855/64–1885/94	2·13	1·33
1860/9–1890/9	2·05	1·17
1865/74–1895/1904	1·98	1·07

SOURCE: [8:*96*].

Hobsbawm and others have drawn between the striking economic growth – which undoubtedly occurred – between the Crimean War and the early seventies, and the less impressive performance of the economy in the preceding decades [1:*6*; 81:*269*]. Absolute increments to output were huge, but Deane's revised figures suggest that, while the secular rate of expansion between 1850 and 1873 was impressive, it was neither spectacular nor very dissimilar from growth in the 1840s[5]; it is interesting that Thomas Tooke, a contemporary statistician and a perceptive commentator on economic matters, omitted to draw unfavourable comparisons between the 1840s and the 1850s, recording his 'unfeigned astonishment' at the 'solidity

and vastness of amelioration in the state of Great Britain'
between 1840 and 1856 [150:*448*].

We may conclude that the secular rate of growth reached its
peak between the 1840s and the 1870s, but that the *difference* in
the rate achieved (important in identifying unifying characteristics) was relatively modest. Thus, although there was a
strong rise in the long-term movement of G.N.P. between 1850
and 1873, compared with trends earlier and later in the century
these growth rates were neither sufficiently spectacular nor distinctive enough to justify attributing to that period a special
and significant unity; the erratic course of economic expansion,
which we consider below, reinforces such a judgement. By the
criterion of price trend we have shown that, if we set aside the
spectacular but short-lived gold-based inflation of 1853–5 and
the cyclical inflationary boom of 1870–3, the most striking
general characteristic is one of high, but relatively stable,
prices, which from the mid-1860s exhibit a mildly deflationary
trend. It will become clear, however, that if we seek to understand the dynamics of the economy the focus should centre
primarily upon relative price movements between and within
sectors and industries. Neither in terms of growth nor price
trend does the mid-Victorian period possess a unity.

3 Domestic Dimensions

(i) INVESTMENT AND STRUCTURAL CHANGE

I T is not difficult to identify the major types of investment which contributed to the mid-Victorian expansion: agriculture, railways, housebuilding, industrial production, overseas trade and capital exports. However, their relative importance throughout the period, their particular characteristics and the role they played in British economic growth, has been the subject of considerable debate to which we now turn. An examination of the disposition of the various components of expenditure generating national product shows fixed domestic capital formation exceeding foreign investment by a substantial margin throughout the 1850s and 1860s (see Table 3).* When private domestic investment fell back from the high peak of the railway construction boom of the mid-1840s, public expenditure associated with the Crimean War more than offset the decline in domestic capital formation, which resumed its upward course in the 1860s and 1870s [152:*114*]. By that time, public current expenditure had fallen from slightly more than 7 per cent to a little more than 5 per cent, probably its lowest level for the nineteenth century [8:*99*]. A breakdown of gross domestic

* Deane's figures exclude stocks and work in progress, and understate the relative magnitudes of domestic capital formation and net foreign investment. Feinstein's estimates take account of these factors, but as they begin only in 1855 we chose to employ Deane's figures, which can be compared with those for other periods; and unless it is stated to the contrary all of our statements are based on these revised estimates. Between 1856 and 1866 Deane's estimates first run above, then below, those of Feinstein, 'but the differences are moderate in absolute terms and the two agree in the mid 60s', after which they diverge [64:*191,193*].

fixed-capital-formation estimates show transport and communications to have accounted for over one-half of the gross capital formation in the 1850s and 1860s. Next in importance, at levels between one-fifth and one-quarter, came social capital (largely dwellings, but also including new hospitals, poorhouses, schools and sanitation systems); in effect, this meant that round about three-quarters of gross domestic fixed-capital-formation expenditures during this period went into constructing the basic infrastructure of a highly industrialised and urbanised economy – the equipment of a transport and communications system and social capital in dwellings and public buildings [8:*99–102*].

Table 3

Home and Overseas Investment: Decadal Averages and Percentages of G.N.P. at Current Market Prices

	Gross Fixed Domestic Capital Formation per cent	Net Foreign Investment per cent
1845–54	6·5	0·9
1850–9	5·4	2·2
1855–66	5·3	2·6
1860–9	5·8	2·9
1865–74	6·3	4·7

SOURCE: [8:*99*].

A distinction is often drawn between the expansion of the fifties, dominated by 'glamorous external developments', and the sixties when 'Britain turned for a time to homely domestic tasks' [23:*23*]. But such a dichotomy is more difficult to justify when it appears that net foreign investment was a lower percentage of gross national product than gross fixed-domestic-capital formation, not only in the 1850s but also in the 1860s, when relatively high foreign investment coincided with already high levels of domestic investment. Overseas trade increased slightly as a proportion of national income throughout the period; the figures were 17·9 per cent for 1855–9, 18·5 per cent for 1860–4, 21·4 per cent for 1865–9, and for 1870–4 22·1 per cent [95:*291*]. The relative importance of domestic and external developments in the two decades was not dissimilar, and while the origins of the boom of the 1860s were domestic, the American Civil War and the consequent Cotton Famine intensified the stimulus to investment in India, Turkey and even South America, in search of alternative supplies of raw cotton.

(a) Agriculture's 'Golden Age'

The agricultural sector, for long held to have experienced a 'golden age' in our period, was still basic to the economy in 1851, when it contributed 20 per cent to national income and accounted for 22 per cent of the nation's labour force. By 1871 these proportions had fallen to 14 per cent income and 15 per cent labour. But these changes reflected the rapid rate of expansion in other sectors, in addition to which the rural exodus brought a reduction in the labour force from 2·1 million to 1·8 million, in part the effect of the pull of higher wages and better conditions in non-farm employment and partly of mechanisation on the farm. Such indicators are not evidence of an ailing sector, for whereas wheat production declined slowly after the Corn Law Repeal in 1846, the output of dairy produce and meat increased substantially, until by the early 1870s the estimated United Kingdom annual average value output of livestock products (£154·8 million) exceeded that of arable products (£94·9 million) [68: *432*].

Of course, the debate over the Corn Laws, with all its political overtones, had suggested a real possibility that the withdrawal of protection might ruin British farmers. But competing demands for grain by other countries, notably continental Europe, the disruption of grain supplies from Russia by war in the Crimea, the high incidence of transport costs from the American interior and the surge of domestic demand for food in the United States following the Civil War, were the long- and short-term factors which together postponed, for more than twenty years, the flood of cheap grain supplies from overseas, and helped to support domestic price levels [61: *562*; 128: *279*; 62: *419*]. After initial fluctuations immediately following Repeal, wheat prices drifted downwards, but slowly enough to enable large, efficient cereal growers located on land best adapted for the purpose, mainly on the light soil districts of south and eastern England, to farm profitably. Hence contraction of wheat production occurred gradually [9:101–5]. Coincident with the modest drop in wheat prices was a sharp rise in the price of livestock products. This was due to the combined effects of population growth, a modest rise in real incomes, becoming marked in the later 1860s, and greater popularity of textiles incorporating wool which, especially during the Cotton Famine of the 1860s, became a common substitute for cotton. The result of these divergent price trends was a relative deterioration in cereal prices, which, by shifting the balance of profitability, stimulated the rearing of animals for store stock in the pasture regions of the north and west; in the south and eastern districts mixed farming received a stimulus, both for cereal growing and livestock [89; 50]. Indeed, as the years passed even within mixed farming the livestock side typically came to assume an increasingly dominant role. Meanwhile this trend towards more intensive mixed farming was promoted further by imports of artificial fertilisers and feedstuffs, which together with important advances in drainage technology improved even the opportunities of the less-advantaged farmers on the heavy clays to adapt to the new structure of farm-product prices. It was these innovations which provided the key to best farming practice publicised as 'high farming' by contemporaries, though its effectiveness depended much upon topographical factors [17].

Partly because of this, and partly because of a lack of appreciation of this vital factor, much of the costly and long-term investment in drainage and new buildings was slow to yield returns, which all too often were absurdly low [148:385–97]. This was partly in the nature of such investment, especially on the less tractable soils, and it may be significant that in East Anglia, in the forefront of agricultural progress for more than a century, landlords were investing a declining proportion of their incomes in fixed capital formation. A corollary was the greater capital burden borne by many tenant farmers in East Anglia, but in this, as in landlords' investment expenditure, that important region was probably an exception [83:441–3]. Elsewhere, landlords appear to have shown a reluctance to raise rents, further weakening their own position and simultaneously strengthening that of tenant farmers in a period when the price of most farm products was rising. Thus, farmers, rather than landowners, prospered in this period, though to what extent we do not know, and farming profits provided the basis for the rise and expansion of an agricultural machinery industry [12:*221–3*]. Uneven in its incidence, nevertheless prosperity on the land also raised the level and trend of rewards to farm labour [31:*95–104*].

Whatever the implications of developments in agriculture for the acute difficulties which were to face rural communities after the mid-seventies, in our period farming structure and organisation proved flexible enough and rural initiative sufficiently positive to effect a partial transformation of the agricultural sector. This brought about an appreciable rise in real output and prosperity [17:*33–4*] at a time when the relative importance of farming was in decline.

(b) Railways, Capitalism and Growth

Railway development, both at home and abroad, provided a substantial, if erratic, stimulus to investment. The question arises, how important economically were the railways? R. Dudley Baxter, writing in 1866, was convinced that 'the very great increase of commerce and national prosperity' of the years since 1842 was due in greater measure to the railways than to free trade, a view which ran counter to much of the popular and informed opinion of his day, which considered free trade to have been the main instrument. 'We ought to give railways their due credit and praise as the chief of those mighty agents which, within the last thirty years have changed the face of civilization' [30:*61*]. He pointed to the growth of trade in England, France, Belgium and the United States, countries with similar cultures, having access to similar steam technology, but only one of which, England, had adopted free trade before 1860. While acknowledging the importance of steam-powered machinery, Baxter argued that it was only after the introduction of steam-powered railways that trading expansion occurred on a rapid and extensive scale, not only as a result of the cost-reducing effects of railways, but also because railways actually created new trade [30: *59–61*]. Indeed, viewed from a different perspective, the railways have been explicitly represented as a critical element in the history of British capitalism. Thus, Checkland has maintained that the depression of the early 1840s was more than a cyclical phenomenon, that it reflected the exhaustion of investment opportunities, and heralded an imminent 'breakdown' of the free-enterprise economy: 'the railway has been the classical capital user of all time; it appeared in its greatest strength in Britain at the very moment when the need was greatest' [5: *17–27*]. Hobsbawm also stressed the critical relationship between the railways and the institutional survival of free-enterprise capitalism in Victorian Britain, at a time in the late 1830s and early 1840s when it is alleged that the system experienced its most acute crisis and when the prospect of economic breakdown of the capitalist order seemed possible [81: *59*]. The railways, he argued, enabled the system to surmount the 'original crisis of the Industrial Revolution'; by diversifying the hitherto narrow productive base the railways launched industrial capitalism into its second phase, broadly based on a foundation of capital-goods production [81: *92*].

The place of the railways in the British economy, with respect in particular to their contribution to economic growth, has been the subject of a recent econometric analysis by Hawke [11]. By employing the concept of social saving, Hawke attempts to measure the cost-reducing effects of the railways. This involves attributing costs to alternative hypothetical methods of transport in a non-rail economy, which in Hawke's model remain those in existence when the railways were introduced. He reckons that the 1865 level of national income of England and Wales was, *at most*, 11 per cent higher as a result of the railways.

Not only does Hawke argue that, though important, railways as providers of transport services made a smaller contribution to the national economy than has been widely assumed, but that the external economic benefits of railways have also been exaggerated. Historians have long recognised that in terms of their contribution to national income the railways' demand for iron was the most significant linkage. On the basis of Mitchell's figures [113: *3*], Hawke calculated that railways absorbed 18 per cent of the U.K. output of pig iron in the peak years of impact 1844–51, a figure which ran at a level of between 8 and 9 per cent in the 1850s and 1860s, though this understates the importance of railway demand for iron by the amount required in the construction of related physical capital stock in the form of rolling stock, components, stations, sheds, bridges and station furniture. He concluded that, while it is unlikely that any other single product was such a large proportion of the iron industry's output, the total output was varied, the proportion of it composed of rails was not overwhelming, and that it is difficult to find gains to non-railway sectors of the economy flowing from railway demand. Railways, he concluded, were not essential to the existence of an iron industry.

Another way of assessing the relative importance of railways in the economic expansion of the period is by considering the income-generating expenditure attributable to that sector. As a proportion of gross fixed domestic capital formation, railway investment averaged between 20 and 25 per cent in the 1850s and 1860s, following the all-time peak of 55 per cent for the quinquennium 1845–9.[6] As a proportion of national income during the late forties railway investment reached 6 per cent, though throughout the 1850s and railway boom of the early 1860s, the figure never again reached 3 per cent [112: *Table 1*]. The high proportion of gross fixed domestic capital formation accounted for by railway investment raises the possibility that, while in terms of its share in national income railway investment was relatively modest (though not in comparison with other sectors), its leverage effect on the economy and its greater volatility enabled the railways to lead in the growth process. Indeed, it seems unlikely, given the structure of the mid-Victorian economy, that any other single innovation could have provided a comparable stimulus. Nevertheless, an examination of the chronology of investment by Mitchell suggests that railways did not lead the economy, rather they played a supporting role, attracting investment funds and speculation only when the state of the capital market was favourable [112: *320*].

This is not the place to rehearse the critical literature which Hawke's findings have generated, important though it is. For, heavily qualified though many of his conclusions and estimates are and notwithstanding the conceptual and substantive criticisms levelled against his research, even within very wide margins of error if Hawke's findings are accepted – and no critic has been prepared to dismiss them as frivolous – his conclusions relating to investment proportions and iron consumption warrant a basic reinterpretation of the view expressed by Checkland and Hobsbawm, namely that the railways constituted a *deus ex machina*, rescuing from an unspecified counterfactual fate a capitalist order which by the early 1840s could not provide enough profitable investment outlets for the capital surplus it generated each year. From the standpoint of the entire economy, runs the argument, they were – by accident rather than by design – an admirable solution to the crisis of the first phase of British capitalism. Hawke's study suggests that without the railways, national income in 1865 might have been up to 11 per cent lower than it actually was; we deduce that the difference would have been less than this in preceding years, for the 11 per cent attributable to railways was only achieved after thirty years of railway economy, a figure which represents a gradual loss roughly equivalent to three or four years' growth in national income. This does not suggest that without the railways a crisis of capitalism would have occurred, either in 1842 or 1848, when social unrest was at its height.

The critical significance which some historians have extended to the railways in the development of capitalism is the notion that the system possessed an inherent instability tending to destroy the capitalist order, and that a surplus of capital was generated within industry and trade which, if railways had not provided an outlet, would have depressed the rate of return on capital below the level at which investors were willing to continue to invest. Economists would describe this as a partial equilibrium statement, which in a general equilibrium context requires extensive elaboration if the hypothesis is to become credible, for it assumes away the probability of alternative patterns of investment which would have become necessary in a non-rail economy. Furthermore, contrary to the opinion of Ward-Perkins [155: *272*], Hawke supports the view expressed by Newmarch in 1857 when he maintained that railway investment in the 1840s required a reduction of consumption and not only a redirection of investment resources, an analysis which

Hawke considers might also have been applicable to the railway boom of the mid-1860s [11:*210*]. The implication is that consumption would have replaced at least a portion of the effective demand generated by railways. Against this argument, which attributes to railways a more modest role, it is true that capital exports, which we stress elsewhere, were closely linked with railway construction overseas, but the exported railway items associated with capital exports have been included in the figures quoted above, and allowed for in Hawke's social-savings figure.

Hobsbawm and Checkland argue that without the railways the level of real investment would have been, in some sense, inadequate for capitalist development. However, Mitchell's estimates caution against the acceptance of the indispensability thesis, not only on account of the proportion of railway iron to total iron production, but also because he shows that diversification within the iron industry pre-dated the railways, the range of iron products in the mid-1830s including water and gas pipes, columns and girders for buildings, chain cables, iron bridges and iron boats. Thus the second phase of diversified industrialism, based on the capital-goods industries, did not depend for its foundation on the railways, though they contributed to it. The industrialisation process would seem to have gained sufficient momentum in Britain, Europe and the United States, to produce a degree of economic expansion which, while undoubtedly lower, could not have been more than temporarily delayed. The capitalist economy faced no fundamental economic crisis in the sense that some have claimed, though as it turned out the railways were, in fact, an important element in mid-Victorian growth.

(c) *Building Construction and Urbanisation*

An important linkage at home which has yet to be thoroughly explored is that between the extension of railways and urban development. This brings us to the second major category of investment, residential and public-building construction, which accounted for between 20 and 25 per cent of gross domestic fixed capital formation from the 1840s, until it rose to more than 30 per cent in the boom of the 1870s [8:*101*]. An index of residential construction for this period shows a rising trend reaching a peak in the mid-seventies, and it was dominated, as we would expect, by housebuilding in urban areas [158: *120–1*]. London housebuilding increased in the later 1850s and early 1860s to the boom of 1868, falling to 1871 and rising with the national trend in the early 1870s. In Liverpool a rising trend in the early 1850s continued more gradually to a peak in 1864, followed by a fall sometime in the late 1860s and early 1870s. Both Cairncross and, more recently, Brinley Thomas have stressed the importance of the links between migration and the level of building investment, explaining the rising trend of the 1850s in terms of heavy internal migration to the towns, as the number of persons employed in agriculture commenced its rapid decline. During the 1860s and 1870s the net urban gain in England and Wales totalled 1·3 million people, representing the same rate of urban growth as in the 1850s. Net emigration settled down to a comparatively low level in the 1850s as industry, and especially transport and trade, absorbed approximately two-thirds of the rural exodus [147:*124–5*; 40:*25*]. While the rate of population growth was slightly lower than in the second quarter of the century, urban migration was greater, providing an important stimulus to the demand for housing. This depended for its effectiveness upon a variety of factors, not the least of which was real income.

Given the close relationship between migration and building, what was the connection with transport, which Isard argued long ago [85:*149*] was a principal determinant of the level of building activity? Inasmuch as the railways caused the relocation of economic activity, they were instrumental in contributing to the greater building activity in those towns affected – the extreme case of this being Crewe – though there were others less directly stimulated, like Barrow, Middlesbrough and Derby [92:*3*]. But in addition to the rise of railway towns, the growth of existing towns was associated with intensified suburban development. Our knowledge is best with respect to London, where two major innovations in transport coincided with the onset of a building boom in the mid-1850s: the first underground railway was sanctioned in 1854 and two years later the London General Omnibus Company expanded and vastly improved the efficiency and cost of its services. In 1861 low-cost workmen's trains were introduced and in 1864 the Board of Trade was empowered to require any railway to provide cheap workmen's trains. Dyos's research on Camberwell shows that by the 1860s it had become one of a new ring of railway suburbs [57]. Thus the London building boom of the 1860s and 1870s has been explained in terms of transport developments, to which the speculative builder contributed to a considerable degree. What was true for London, however, though important because of its relative position in the total housing supply, may not have been true for other towns. In Glasgow, for example, Cairncross has shown that the mechanism at work was that which related the lack of economic activity in the region to building investment. Here, investment in shipbuilding explained the chronology of residential construction, for the high levels of employment associated with industrial expansion encouraged marriage, migration, and led to a fall in the number of unoccupied houses; hence a rise in housebuilding [39:21–2]. Parry Lewis found that a similar mechanism operated in Manchester and South Wales, where the prosperity of local industry exerted its impact through rising wages and migration into those areas [20:129]. Building, therefore, is seen as an important component of gross fixed-domestic-capital formation which is dependent upon another of similar magnitude, namely industrial capital, which tended to move in phase [8:101, Table 4]. The Weber index of residential construction identifies a peak in building activity pervading major cities in 1863, but provides scant support for the existence of a U.K. building cycle before 1870 [158:112–13].

It has been suggested that the striking economic growth of the mid-Victorian period, described as a most remarkable period of capital formation, was directly related to high levels of investment, which contemporary estimates put at around 16 per cent or more of national income [1:6]. But recent calculations suggest that while the level of domestic and foreign investment rose by one or two percentage points, from about 5 per cent in the 1830s and early 1840s to approximately 7 per cent in the railway boom of the late 1840s, the level did not exceed 11 per cent in our period (of which domestic capital formation accounted for less than 7 per cent).[7] Neither was the level of investment in the mid-Victorian boom very different from that in the so-called Great Depression [8: *Table 3*] when the rate of growth of industrial production slowed down. It was not until the early 1860s that investment rose to the level which some economists once suggested was necessary for the 'take-off' stage in industrialisation.

Indeed, for those who, like Hicks, regard the switch to fixed capital associated with the emergence of machine tools as the essential novelty in the Industrial Revolution [79: *147–8*], it is arguable that concentration upon the eighteenth and early nineteenth centuries has distorted our perspective, for the switch to capital-intensive machine-tool production occurred between 1830 and the 1850s [36: *236*]. Added to these factors was the coincidence, in our period, of a marked shift in industrial structure. In terms of the changing structure of national product the percentage of national income attributable to manufacture, mining and building (excluding housing) moved upwards between 1851 and 1871, after two decades of relative stability. The share of trade and transport rose too, but was only slightly more than one-half the proportion (58 per cent) accounted for by manufacturing, mining and building. The gain by these two sectors was chiefly at the expense of the agricultural sector which fell from 20 to 14 per cent between 1851 and 1871, a trend which was to accelerate in the 1870s [56: *6*]. The rapid reduction in the agricultural labour force, a huge expansion in steam-powered factory production, and acceleration in the rate of urbanisation, together mark the emergence of an urban industrial economy and society.

Thus it appears that relatively low levels of investment, expressed as a percentage of national product, were sufficient to achieve annual rates of economic growth which, though in aggregate at something less than 3 per cent, or 2 per cent a head, were the highest for the nineteenth century (see Table 2, p. 24 above). Far from pointing to a rise in the capital–output ratio in this period as has been suggested [126: *197*], this combination of modest investment levels with a rising rate of economic growth suggests that capital–output ratios were falling; that the proportion of national income it was necessary to devote to capital investment in order to raise national income by a given magnitude fell. Partial confirmation of this conclusion is provided by Feinstein's recently published capital–output ratio estimates, though unfortunately his figures begin only in 1855. They show a steadily, if slowly, declining trend in the ratio, which moved slightly upwards once, briefly, between 1855 and 1875 [64: *Table 51*].

In the industrial sector, where the explanation for this is most likely to be found, Blaug has shown that in the cotton industry, at least after 1860, the average productivity of capital began to rise as the result of capital-saving improvements [33: *360–9*]. The empirical basis for confirmation of the aggregate numerical estimates is thin, but there is evidence of a rise in output per worker though again the numerical estimates relate only to the period beginning in 1855 [64: *Table 20*]. Rising labour productivity also helps to explain why the rising proportion of national income attributable to manufacture, mining and building, was not matched by a comparable rise in the proportion of the labour force in that sector. It increased by less than one percentage point between 1851 and 1881, while the trade and transport sector increased its share by more than 5 per cent [56: *Table 30*]. In contrast with slowly rising capital investment and labour inputs, industrial production grew, rapidly, though with some signs of deceleration; a 'climacteric' perhaps from the late 1860s. Even so, the increments to industrial output were enormous in absolute terms and before exploring the origins of the climacteric, therefore, we shall proceed to analyse the character and internal mechanisms of this massive industrial thrust.

The domestic dimensions of British economic development we have reviewed so far highlight the important structural changes which occurred. The third quarter of the century witnessed the beginnings of marked agricultural decline, relative in terms of output values but absolute with respect to labour. But in comparison with trends from the late 1870s the 'golden age' does not seem an inappropriate description, though its lustre was less apparent both to those farmers on land ill-suited or those lacking in initiative to adapt to the new price trends, and to landlords whose investment in this period yielded scant pecuniary return. Rural depopulation was causally related to the growth of towns and high levels of building construction, a major category of gross domestic-capital formation, though this was dependent primarily upon industrial growth. The largest component of capital formation, however, was transport, and railway investment, which was the major part, provided a powerful contribution to economic growth. Hungry for capital, railway investment was an important factor in raising the level of capital formation in the early 1860s to the allegedly critical 'take-off' figure of 10 per cent, by which time the economy had achieved its maximum secular rate of growth. Whether railway investment was a necessary condition for continued economic growth from the 1840s is problematical, and not only because the question is hypothetical. For the degree to which industrialisation and the development of a capital-goods sector had already established a firm foundation for continuing development, and the tendency for railway investment to lag behind the economy's growth momentum, together suggest that the survival of industrial capitalism was due less to the railways than to the basic resilience of the industrial sector, which now requires our careful consideration.

(ii) INDUSTRY AND ECONOMY

(a) Springs of Growth: Origins of Climacteric

The mid-Victorian period is often seen as a time to which industrialists were to look back nostalgically from the vantage point of the so-called Great Depression, when they were swept effortlessly along by the swelling tide of free trade and expanding overseas markets [106:97]. Two points are worth making. Throughout the voluminous evidence presented by manufacturers and merchants before the Royal Commission in the 1880s, the years remembered by most as a time of boom were those between 1868 and 1873 following a period in the mid-1860s variously described by witnesses as one of 'normality' or gradual economic progress. The decade as a whole was regarded with mixed and varied feelings by the diverse organisations of employers and trade unionists representing the various

39

industries and regions. Thus when unfavourable comparisons were drawn between profits in the 1880s and an earlier period, the basis for comparison was the colossal cyclical boom of the early 1870s and the years immediately preceding it. Those who gave evidence were not looking back to what has since become known as the Great Victorian Boom but to much shorter spells, the halcyon years differing between sectors, industries and regions.

Investment and production depend upon profit, and it is unfortunate that the available evidence about profitability is defective in the extreme. Contemporary tax returns indicate a rise in average business profits of about 60 per cent between 1850 and 1880 [101:*58*], but this exaggerates the increase, for the figures are uncorrected for price changes and conceal temporal and sectoral differences. Feinstein's estimates suggest that neither in industrial income (wages and profits) nor in national income was the share of profits more than 2 or 3 per cent higher in the 1860s than in the 1880s [136:*42*], when manufacturers were voluble in their complaints on this matter. We have seen that our period has been commonly described as one of rising prices, whether rapid and sustained, as in some of the older textbooks, or, as in the revised version according to Landes, a short sharp rise, followed by stability or mild deflation. The view that price inflation brought larger profits which in turn generated industrial expansion has been expressed many times, both by historians and economists, and originates in Hamilton's thesis on the origins of the Industrial Revolution [78], since discredited by Felix [65:*441–2*]. The theoretical justification of this argument can be found in Keynes's *A Treatise on Money*, where the stress is on the lag of wage costs behind rising prices, which accelerates capital formation from the greater profits which result. Thus, expectations of price increases are held to encourage investment, in contrast with the discouragement allegedly induced by anticipation of deflation.

The profit-inflation thesis may be construed as a special case of profit expansion, the latter taking into account cost components other than wages which, like labour costs, are assumed to be less volatile than the prices of the finished articles [142:*app.1*]. This assumption was not valid for the late eighteenth century [65:*141–2*], and neither was it for the mid-nineteenth century. For while there is reason to suppose that wages lagged in the initial upward surge of prices, raw-material prices tended to rise faster than the prices of manufactured goods, or fall relatively more slowly (see Table 1, p. 15 above). A rapidly expanding market is not necessarily an indication that profit margins were widening, for these were variables which depended to a large extent on the price elasticity of demand for the finished goods, on the cost structure in different industries, and on the possibility and extent of mechanisation to offset pressures on profit margins. We would emphasise that any conclusions to be drawn, however tentative, rest upon the existence of observed differentials in price movements, and only detailed research on the profitability and conduct of Victorian business will confirm or refute the suggestion that pressures on unit profits provided an important stimulus to technical progress and economic growth.

In those industries, like textiles, where raw materials accounted for a substantial proportion of total costs and the major percentage of variable costs,[8] the squeeze on unit profit could be greater than in an industry like engineering where labour cost was a relatively large component.[9] However, in cotton textiles rising material costs were offset, for the installation stage of self-acting mules and power looms gave way to the operational phase in which rising labour productivity was accompanied by a cut in the capital costs per unit of output [33: *366–7*]. Indeed, figures quoted by Ellison indicate that the cost of cotton as a percentage of the value of output increased between the 1840s and the 1880s [58:*69*]. A similar innovative process in response to rising raw-material prices can be identified in the woollen and worsted industries, where innovations in quality and style of worsteds by the introduction of cotton warps, lowered costs, and by making available wool-based products at prices lower than relatively expensive all-woollen worsteds tapped a new and rapidly expanding overseas demand [74]. Woollen manufacturers tackled a similar problem by varying the proportions of virgin wool to shoddy and mungo. These developments were supported by Lister and Donisthorpe's invention of mechanical woolcombing. Just as machinery in cotton manufacturing had been improved and run at faster speeds, so similar progress was made, first in worsteds then in woollens. Vertically integrated mills were also established, though these were more important in worsted than in woollen manufacture [144:*118*]. In the linen industry the price of flax and the search for alternative sources of supply dominated much of the discussion about the industry's difficulties in the 1850s. The results for those enterprising firms which responded to the need for cost reduction could be buoyant profits and relatively high rates of return on capital employed. Where enterprise was lacking, however, survival in the face of commercial crises was problematical and even innovating firms, for example, in steel and hosiery, were also subject to high mortality rates [133:*244–7*; 60:*165, 184*]. In the silk industry manufacturers faced rising new silk prices until the mid-1860s after which they moved steadily downwards because of the opening of Asiatic production and the effect, from 1869, of the opening of the Suez Canal. Profit margins probably fell in the 1850s, but rose substantially to a peak in the early 1870s when the fall in silk prices, the main determinant of silk production costs, was well established [49:*138–9*]. The rise in silk prices is explained by a physical shortage of silk, and the same is true of rags, which accounted for about 50 per cent of production costs in the manufacture of paper in the 1850s and early 1860s [48:*331–44*]. In the boot and shoe industry the introduction of the sewing machine coincided in the 1850s with rapidly rising leather and hide prices [46:*41*].

A characteristic feature of conditions in the important textile sector was a pull to investment and expanded output resulting partly from a growth in the price-elastic demand for textiles, both in the industrialising and newly developing countries. On the other hand, there was an incentive for manufacturers in this highly competitive sector simultaneously to invest and expand output in order to offset the effects of the growth in demand upon inelastic supplies of textile fibres. Larger outputs could reduce overheads, a component of capital costs which Ellison's figures [58:*61*] show to have been large for the cotton industry. Faced with rising prices of their raw materials, manufacturers invested in known innovations and in new technologies, but this increased productive capacity and intensified competitive pressures. This was true for the cotton industry virtually throughout the entire period, for woollen and worsted yarn manufacturers in the expansion phases in the 1850s, and for cloth producers expansion continued until the late 1860s. The difference reflected the greater possibilities for technical progress in the manufacture of cloth, which was the process furthest from the raw material [74]. The problems of material supply led to the emergence of associations of merchants and manufacturers anxious to solve them, either through substitution or by finding alternative supply sources, notably India for cotton and flax. The tentative conclusion can be drawn that the high rate of industrial growth, at least in the most important sector, textiles, was associated not only with expanding markets but also with a squeeze on profit margins and intense competition, which stimulated investment in cost-reducing innovations in the hope of long-run improvement in profitability [12: *79,100*; 74].

Such a relationship between raw-material prices and final products hardly existed in the other important industrial sectors, iron and steel, shipbuilding, engineering and ferrous-metal manufacturing [12:*140,182*]. These industries relied on domestic resources, principally iron and coal. Hughes argues that the domestic market was the main factor determining investment in iron, while fluctuations in foreign demand were reflected by changes in output, and that investment occurred in periods of rising prices, which in the non-textile sectors coincided with the full utilisation of capacity. Textiles and iron shared the problems of excess capacity resulting from the investment which accompanied the 1851–3 trade boom and the Crimean War, but technical progress had reduced real costs to the extent that, despite high raw-material prices, capacity was again fully employed by the late 1850s, when the recovery of overseas markets prompted further investment. Because investment in iron shipbuilding and some branches of engineering was 'lumpy', the huge expansion of the mid-1850s, due in part to the Crimean War, left those industries with excess capacity until the early 1860s when demand caught up, partly under the stimulus of the American Civil War [12: *219*].

43

There are resemblances, also, in the development of the vitally important coal industry. Between 1850 and 1870 the volume of coal output doubled, although the number of miners (whose working hours declined) rose by barely one-third [146:*49*]. Thus, rising labour productivity, due principally to innovation in ventilation and methods of raising and handling coal, was a major factor countering the tendency, characteristic of mining enterprise, towards diminishing returns, by reducing coal-getting costs [146:*57–8*]. But the relationship between falling costs and relatively stable prices from the mid-1850s is not that of simple cause and effect. Lower transport costs, brought about by the railways, destroyed those regional monopolies which until the late 1840s had dominated the coal trade and especially the supply of the huge London market [6:*301–2*; 11:*396–7*]. The upward acceleration of coal prices in 1852–4 triggered innovative investment in new pits and the enlargement of existing mines. This occurred both in traditional and newer coal-producing regions, notably the great northern coalfields and the steam-coal districts of South Wales [12:*143–9*]. The opening up of the inland coalfields in the 1850s intensified the rapid expansion of capacity that occurred in response to a growing demand from iron, metal-processing and other manufacturing industries [6:*301–2*; 56:*218–20*]. Such was the combination of factors which after the mid-1850s pushed prices down to pre-inflation levels, where they remained until the late 1860s (see Table 1, p. 15 above). Prices which, relative to price movements for most other commodities, were low, partially offset gains from investment and greater labour efficiency – productivity factors which became even more necessary for the survival of colliery enterprise in this new competitive era.

It is difficult to tell how far the interpretation of the dynamics of economic growth in the 1850s and early 1860s can be extrapolated for the entire period, especially as the Civil War introduced vast short-term distortions in the textile industries, which also had long-run implications. Expectations of a return to pre-war cotton prices and especially to higher finished-goods prices as demand expanded, led to increased investment in fixed capital and the expansion of capacity in the cotton industry

[74]. But this expectation proved to be optimistic, for the substitution of mainly wool-based textiles for cotton meant that the consumption of cotton goods in Britain did not exceed the 1860 figure for the remainder of the century [151: *103*]. As for the rest of the textile sector, the incentives to substitute mixed woollens, worsteds and linens for high-priced cotton goods produced a boom in the 1860s which continued, though more moderately, after the Civil War, indicating that the price conditions obtained during the war years both supported and initiated changes in fashion to the benefit of linen and worsted manufacturers. On the other hand, by stimulating the demand for cotton, woollen and linen tissues, the war intensified the raw-material problems facing manufacturers, and by the end of the decade, due partly to an increased supply of sheep and partly to higher yields of Australian fleeces, wool prices fell off. As cotton prices moved downwards too, competition between worsted and cotton manufacturers intensified, for both sections had invested heavily in plant and new machinery in the mid-1860s, often accompanied by changes in organisation [74].

War had some similar effects upon the iron, steel and ship-building industries, partly associated with armaments supply, the shift from wooden sailing ships to iron steamships, and large-scale investment in railways. Here again, as with the 1851–4 boom, investments left excess capacity which awaited the greater boom of the 1870s for absorption and justification for further capital investment. Among the more potent stimulants in this connection were the capital needs of the Americans, supplied by Britain, to resume large-scale railway construction interrupted by the war; hence the British investment in American securities on a large scale at the close of the Civil War. In the boom of the late 1860s strengthened demand for steamships followed the opening of the Suez Canal, while the French War indemnity of £220 million to Germany, with the subsequent boom in Central Europe, added further stimulus to British trade to that area, especially in the supply of iron, steel and coal [7: *264–5*].

The greatest inventions of the mid-Victorian period were the combing machine in the worsted industry and in iron and steel the vitally important Bessemer process, which marked the beginnings of bulk production of this immensely critical material. In 1866, the Siemens–Martin open-hearth process further improved British steel technology, still based on non-phosphoric ores. In the mechanical-engineering industry key inventions, such as the turret lathe, milling and grinding machines, contributed to widen the range of machine tools available to British and foreign industries, and their greater precision and speed were vastly improved by Whitworth's achievements in the design of machine tools, measurement, standardisation and machine practice. The diffusion of technology across a wide range of British industries, the application on a large scale of steam-powered machinery of greater speed and accuracy, also affected many of the finished-metal trades, as well as the textile and other sectors. This vast expansion of capacity at a time when Britain dominated world markets was to exacerbate the problems of adjustment to foreign competition which, even in the mid-Victorian period, was causing some observers concern. Indeed some historians have claimed to identify a turning-point, or 'climacteric', in the British economy sometime during the 1860s [2:407]. What is the evidence?

Certainly some contemporary observers viewed the mid-sixties, especially after the crisis of 1866, with apprehension [163:114–15]. In 1868 the *Edinburgh Review* carried Goschen's famous essay on an 'era of two per cent' in which he expressed the view that capital had gone on strike, because at such a low interest rate investors were not coming forward [2:406]. In the mid-1860s the consol yields and the yield on railway stock both reached their secular peaks and began their long decline – as did prices; in association with the crisis of 1866 Bank Rate reached 10 per cent for the last time before 1914 [12:237]. Cooney has implied that the crisis of 1866 was critical since the boom of the mid-1860s derived its major impetus from railway investment, at a time when the cotton industry was in difficulties. Accepting the verdict of *The Economist* he maintained that it shook the credit system more than any panic since 1847, and that it led to a revision of even long-term investment decisions in favour of foreign investment [7:277]. Hughes stressed the importance of the entry of American goods into international markets, the rise in American output being accompanied by a fall in American prices. A plausible effect, he argued, was a justifiable weakening of the expected yields to British investment [12:*237*]. Both Cooney and Hughes consider the commerical crisis of 1866 as an important historical turning-point, both regarding as exceptional, 'a bubble', the gigantic boom beginning in 1869.

To identify the mid-1860s as a time when prices and interest rates began their long-term downward movement is not the same as locating a climacteric for the economy; indeed the deceleration of home-produced national income, it is now generally agreed, occurred later and the maximum secular growth rate was maintained until the mid-1870s. Nevertheless, if the origins of several long-term changes can be located simultaneously in the 1860s, this strengthens the interpretation of this decade, because of such a conjuncture, as having peculiar importance in nineteenth-century economic history. The cotton famine distorts the long-term pattern because the Hoffman output index puts the cotton industry's output at 30 per cent below the average for 1854–60. The weighting of the industry is sufficiently high (about 18 per cent of the total) for the effect to produce a significant check to the rate of growth in the average index, whereas the intercyclical growth rate for the succeeding periods was raised by the relatively high growth rate in cotton, as output recovered from an abnormally low level. The removal of cotton has the effect that the sharp break in the intercyclical measures of productivity growth occurs in the period ending 1866–74, rather than that ending 1875–83, which led Coppock [51:*9*] to suggest that the origins of the general decline may be found in the late 1860s (see Table 4).

The statistics lack precision, while the effects of the Civil War and the exceptional European boom make it difficult to identify trends with certainty. None the less, the apparent decline in output per head seems to warrant a brief review of qualitative evidence on mid-Victorian industrial performance. Furthermore, whether the 1860s were more, or less, successful, in terms of industrial achievement, than the 1850s is important in the present context for the light it could throw upon the debate over entrepreneurship in the later nineteenth century; in particular the contention that both were decades of business euphoria, when the workshop of the world became the cradle of late-Victorian complacency.

(b) Enterprise and Euphoria

While international industrial predominance was undisputed, the challenge to British superiority was growing perceptibly. The various voluminous reports on international industrial exhibitions in London, Paris and Vienna illuminated weaknesses as well as strengths, and even in the 1850s some textile

Table 4

Intercyclical Average Annual Growth Rates Including and Excluding Building and Cotton Textiles

	Industrial Production Excluding Building	Productivity	Productivity Corrected for Unemployment
1847/53–1854/60	3·5 (3·0)	2·4 (2·1)	2·4[a] (2·1[a])
1854/60–1861/5	1·7 (3·5)	0·6 (2·3)	0·6 (2·3)
1861/5–1866/74	3·6 (2·8)	2·4 (1·3)	2·2 (1·1)
1866/74–1875/83	2·1 (2·1)	0·9 (0·6)	1·0 (0·7)
1875/83–1884/9	1·6 (1·6)	0·2 (0·0)	0·5 (0·3)

NOTE: Figures in brackets refer to average growth rate excluding building *and* cotton textiles.

[a] uncorrected.

SOURCE: [51:*7–8*].

manufacturers demonstrated an awareness that effective foreign competition was a fact, would intensify, and would require appropriate entrepreneurial response [143:*31*]. This was also the picture in hosiery and lace [66:*422,735*], while glass manufacturers had already lost a large share of the domestic market for window glass to Belgian producers [28:*136–7*]. A similar message of impending challenge was relayed in the 1850s by those who were overwhelmed during their inspection of mechanised factories in the United States, where metal goods, screws, files, clocks, watches and small arms, reapers and some workshop machinery were produced with standardised interchangeable parts [37:*135*]. A few years later, Sheffield was losing the important American market for heavy tools, saws, cheap cutlery and files [125:*126-7*], while in Birmingham and the Black Country manufacturers complained that free trade had failed to produce the anticipated boom in hardware [149: *89,94,125,608,615,642,658*]. Iron and steel manufacturers were accused of resting on their oars, of indifference to the dissemination of technical information and the lack of a scientific approach to production [38:*ch.1*]; but the picture was by no means uniformly unfavourable [42:*45*]. Yet it was in the middle of the nineteenth century, according to Alfred Marshall, that 'an unprecedented combination of advantages enabled businessmen to make money, even when they were not throwing themselves with energy into that creative work by which industrial leadership is made and maintained'. It is alleged that during this period 'rich old firms could thrive by their mere momentum even if they had lost the springs of energy and initiative', and that irrespective of entrepreneurial effectiveness the tide of inflation was so great that in most cases the weak, as well as the strong, made good profits and were satisfied with themselves. 'Thus an extraordinary combination of favourable conditions induced self-complacency – the arch enemy of strength' [106: *87,92-3*].

Apart from the elementary fact that as industry expanded the rich old firms were declining as a proportion of the total population of firms, without a noticeable increase in business concentration, there is some evidence to suggest that Marshall's generalisations concerning price inflation, profits and businessmen, which are deeply rooted in the historiography of this period, require considerable qualification. We have already alluded to the pressures and conditions of uncertainty surrounding rapid innovation in the textile industries at that time, which hardly supports the view that the mid-Victorian entrepreneurs were easyriders, or likely, on the basis of experience in this period, to have succumbed to such a myopic philosophy. Indeed Hughes's impression based on his research into the 1850s was that perhaps the most important factor accounting for the impressive record of economic growth was 'the spirit of risk (or perhaps even speculation) which prevailed in the British economy, in which specific industries suffered time and time again from excess capacity, careless investment, and the consequent periodic wave of failures' [12:*288–9*]. To the pressures facing the textile manufacturers, especially after 1860, we might have added that of the devastating effect of free trade on the Coventry ribbon manufacturers [129:*122*], but it is also possible to point to difficulties experienced by other groups.

Ironmasters in Staffordshire, Shropshire and South Wales were exercised by the effects of the phenomenal rise of the Middlesbrough iron industry based on Cleveland ores [42:*78–82*]. In the Black Country the situation of many iron-manufacturing firms has been judged 'distinctly insecure' and several failed [32:*156*]. Perhaps the most spectacular failure in the industry, however, occurred in 1864 with the liquidation of the Derwent Iron Company, the largest in England, which was transformed by its new owners into the highly profitable Consett Iron Company [132:*71*]. The investment booms associated with war in each decade intensified the amplitude in iron and coal producers' outputs. After the price inflation and investment boom of the early 1850s coal prices dropped to pre-inflation levels, which in the opinion of the Select Committee 'did not afford a reasonable profit to the owners of collieries'. Prominent figures familiar with the industry in the north and north-eastern coalfields were convinced that both for those who owned and operated collieries it was not until the early 1870s that return on capital was satisfactory.[10] Following the investment boom associated with the Crimean War, shipbuilding on the Thames deteriorated, and by the mid-1860s the production of iron vessels in the north of England had begun to provide serious competition. The 1866 commercial crisis which brought down a number of shipbuilders, pushed the Thames shipbuilders into severe and lasting depression [124:*78–82*]. Beginning in the late forties, within a decade competition in the glass industry virtually eliminated further production in the nation's major centre on the Tyne [28:*119–20*]. The leather crisis of 1860 precipitated the collapse of no fewer than thirty leather firms [97:*225*], and in the boot and shoe industry those firms which did not innovate in the 1850s and 1860s had perished by 1871 [46:*43*]. Meanwhile, Scottish papermakers suffered in the aftermath of free trade and were slow to recover [39:*95*]. This general picture is not intended to represent the course of British industrial change, but to ensure caution against oversimplification, and to underline the regional basis of the mid-Victorian boom. It is offered as evidence that entrepreneurs encountered problems of adjustment arising out of competition and technological change, and that even within an overall context of economic expansion investment was accompanied by risk. Entrepreneurial inertia and difficulties of relocation often resulted in business failure,[11] especially during the commercial crises of the period [97:*243–4*].

Lack of data prevents confirmation that profitability, or rate of return, in our period greatly exceeded that in preceding decades[12] or during the years of the so-called Great Depression, but it is worth noting that in the 1860s John Watts, a knowledgeable industrial observer, stated that average profits *normally* regarded as satisfactory in the cotton trade were about 12½ per cent [156:*342*], which is only slightly less than the figure for profit on capital employed at the sizeable Ashworth cotton enterprise between 1854 and 1879 [34:*68*]. Phelps Brown and Weber have produced estimates of a 15 per cent aggregate rate of return for the entire industrial sector between 1879 and 1900 [123:*287*], and while we must be cautious in drawing any conclusions from such disparate and ill-defined data, the relatively small difference in the order of magnitude suggests that until this problem has been researched we should remain sceptical of the belief that in comparison with the later decades the large industrial profits of the mid-nineteenth century were related to exceptionally high profitability.

Even if mid-Victorian optimism had been the disease of British businessmen, it does not appear to have infected investors (often business organisations) in stocks and shares. For, unreliable though it may be for analysis of short-term movements, Rousseaux's share-price index may be adequate for a study of long waves in speculation, and thus indicative of confidence [71:*457–8*]. This shows an annual rate of increase of less than 3 per cent in share prices between 1851 and 1871. Only in the speculative boom of the early 1860s does the index reveal a strong upward movement, only to be reversed, though temporarily and to levels above those of the 1850s, in 1864. The lack of a sustained bullish trend does not support the view of the middle decades as years of unusual confidence and optimism. At a more general level, Checkland has drawn attention to the juxtaposition of self-assurance and self-doubt in the middle-class Victorian mind at this time, not least due to recurrent, real fears of bottleneck scarcity [44:57].

(c) Trend and Cycle

One clue to the mind of the business community is suggested by the reflections of the Council of the Birmingham Chamber of Commerce, whose members did not think they were experiencing the beginnings of a long-term erosion of industrial supremacy in the 1860s, even though Birmingham metal manufacturers were already at that time feeling the effects of competition. Neither did they seem to be impressed by the support derived by the economy from what was probably the first peak of a long swing in housebuilding investment in 1863 which coincided with a similar rising wave of capital exports, culminating in a peak in the early 1870s boom. Two years after the commercial crisis of 1866, reference was made to the 'long continued depression' which was seen as part of the normal 'ebb and flow of economic life; if we would take wisdom from the past and avoid the trying times of depression in future, we must prevent the previous expansion which causes them' [161:223–4]. It was suggested that the memories of businessmen would lead them to pronounce that they were then approaching an equilibrium. In 1876 a report reviewing trading conditions referred to 'recurring periods of activity and dullness which have been the experience of many years . . . and if the present depression is of longer duration and greater severity than usual it is due to causes that it is hoped may be proved exceptional' [161:268]. The reference here was to the preceding hectic boom associated with the Franco-Prussian War, which Sheffield industrialists had called 'the great inflation' [125:125]. Thus, while Goschen might write about the 'strike of capital' from 1866, businessmen probably thought in terms of short-term changes in opportunities. Volatile raw-material prices, whether in textiles, leather, rubber or soap manufacture, required close attention to short-term fluctuations if costs were to be contained or gains secured.[13] It is less surprising, therefore that entrepreneurs should be influenced strongly by short-term and cyclical phenomena in our period.

It was Redford's impression that even in the 1850s Manchester businessmen 'cannot for long have been free from the fear of commercial collapse lurking behind each temporary revival of trade' [130:*xxii*]. There is abundant evidence to support Redford's view of the mid-Victorian decades, for despite the upward trend in textiles of capacity, production and trade, even in the 1850s the years of adversity seemed to be as numerous as those of prosperity, the narrowing of profit margins at times creating real difficulties for the business community [12:*76*]. The uncertainties of the 1860s, especially in the cotton trade, are well established [23:*380–1*]. For the economy as a whole, a statistical analysis of the duration and amplitude of cycles in G.N.P. also shows that of the twenty-eight years between 1846 and 1874, fifteen years were in upswing and thirteen in downswing, compared with fifteen years' upswing and eleven in downswing in the period 1875–1901. There was no marked change in amplitude or intensity of cycles during the second half of the century [25:*9*]. This suggests that it is misleading to extend the exhilaration surrounding the Great Exhibition of 1851 to the two decades which followed at least as far as the expectations of businessmen are concerned – and hence their propensity to invest.

This raises a further question concerning the relationship between secular trends and fluctuations in economic activity. For if we are correct in thinking that businessmen were influenced more in their decision-making at this time by short-run, rather than long-term, factors, quite understandably in the context of an uncontrolled, unstable, free-enterprise capitalist system, then contrary to common assumption long-term economic trends were at least in part the outcome of short-term fluctuations. After the commercial crisis of 1866, accompanied by financial disasters, bankruptcy and a marked increase in unemployment [141:*3*; 7:*265*; 53], the mania type of investment, culminating in a crisis, ceased to be a feature of the

53

economy and it may well be that this kind of investment buoyancy which seems to have diminished in the late 1870s and 1880s, when net foreign investment began to dominate secular fluctuation [70:*30*], is partly related to change in the institutional structure.

Though the organisation of commerce and the speeding up of communications in this period reduced some of the risks of trading, and in particular virtually eliminated inventory fluctuations [6:*312–18*], intense competition and falling profit margins in the mid-nineteenth century could force even the more respectable merchants to relax precautions on exchange dealings, and in effect increase the risk factor in the commercial sector [94:*10*]. The joint-stock limited-liability legislation of 1855–62 did not prove to be a stabilising influence in business during its early years of operation. Integrated joint-stock banking had developed since 1826, accompanied by the establishment of banks with overdraft facilities which reduced the demand for money for inventory financing; but the banking habit among the general public grew slowly and it was not until the 1870s that inland bills, a major source of instability, declined to a significant extent [22:*78*]. In our period the bill was an important element both of growth and instability, because the magnitude of bill creations was determined by the level of trade and businessmen's expectations, which meant that the growth of the bill structure accelerated the boom and in its collapse augmented the violence of the contraction [12:*274*]. But after the booms, crises and liquidations, the bill-supported credit left tangible results in the form of permanent plant and equipment whose construction was justified by the high levels of output credit expansion allowed, just as earlier share-market manias had produced permanent economic gains. Underpinning the booms of this period was the Bank of England's tactical procedure for dealing, combining its activities as a private profit-making venture with that of acting as a bank of last resort for the business community. This was achieved, after the 1847 crisis, by allowing Bank Rate to *follow* rates in the discount market, in effect leaving business to set the level of economic activity in crisis situations [13:*230–1*].

We can be less sure of the influence of changes in the importance of fixed investment in manufacturing upon stability before the 1870s. Habakkuk has argued that the spread of factory industry at the expense of domestic industry in most cases caused a shift to fixed capital from working capital, and that an increase of the more capital-intensive, at the expense of the less capital-intensive, meant that fluctuations in the rate of capital formation assumed greater significance as a source of fluctuation [76:269]. Estimates of the proportion of industrial capital to gross domestic-capital formation, and of the latter to gross national product, do not indicate any marked upward trend and do not afford support to that thesis [8], but we suggest, nevertheless, that the elements of instability had not been substantially reduced before 1870, that for our period they were strengthened by the random shocks of two wars and intense political uncertainty [100], that the extraneous circumstances which made for speculative manias and violent booms were favourable to the creation of capacity, and that the increase of new techniques acquired in this way outweighed the fact that some investment was misdirected because it was made under the influence of short-term considerations [76:272]. In each of the investment booms of the 1850s and 1860s the market was favourable to innovation which enlarged productive capacity, but these were often introduced when profit margins were under pressure as entrepreneurs appear to have responded by expanding capacity and innovations. This analysis is congruent with Hughes's observation that the rate of economic growth in the period depended largely upon the strength and duration of the booms, which in turn he saw as the product of a 'dynamic, but unstable economy populated by risk-taking entrepreneurs' [12:288–9].

While mid-Victorian growth was striking, it is misleading to assume that it was also a period of profit inflation, easy gain and entrepreneurial euphoria. In the largest industrial sector – textiles – price and cost relationships reinforced by intense competition, stimulated innovation, investment, expansion and profit fluctuations. The artificial stimulus of war demands produced similar complex discontinuous developments in iron, shipbuilding and coal. Overall, the period brought alternating, but not all simultaneous, spells in most industries of high and low levels of output, employment and profits, while technical changes added problems of industrial relocation to these difficulties. Such a situation was hardly conducive to general entrepreneurial complacency, notwithstanding British industrial pre-eminence in her quasi-monopoly position; to subscribe to that notion is to commit a fallacy of composition. Furthermore, by the 1860s weaknesses were being explored and publicised, heralding the inevitable intensification of competition with emerging industrial countries, especially as the post-war American economy swung into high industrial gear. Meanwhile, changes in the trend of prices, interest rates, net imports of manufactures and industrial productivity suggest that the mid-1860s mark an important economic watershed, the commercial crisis of 1866 ending the cyclical dynamism which was characteristic of mid-Victorian industrial capitalism and arguably essential to unprecedented levels of economic growth.

4 External Dimensions

S O far we have stressed the domestic factors which contributed
to the mid-Victorian economic expansion, but the growth of
capital exports and a phenomenal increase in overseas trade
were also of central importance. As a proportion of national
income, trade rose rapidly, but unsteadily, to reach a peak at
22 per cent in the early 1870s. Throughout this time exports
acted as a leading sector, drawing resources from the under-
employed, low-productivity sectors, notably agriculture, to
more productive employment. We should avoid the danger,
however, of regarding exports as the only independent variable,
with capital formation and consumption dependent upon them
[95:*213*]. Superior machine technology and factory organisation gave British manufacturing industry a comparative
advantage, enabling her to supply the rest of the world with a
vast range of textiles at relatively low cost, to supply iron,
machinery and railway equipment of high quality in quantities
required by other countries, especially those which were themselves undergoing the process of industrialisation. Over 80 per
cent of home-produced exports in this period were manufactured goods, of which textiles contributed about 70 per cent (or
more than 60 per cent of the total) in the 1850s and 1860s,
only a slightly lower proportion than in the earlier decades.
The falling share is explained by the growing proportion of
exports attributable to iron and steel manufactures, machinery
and rolling stock. Among other sizeable export categories were
cotton, woollen and silk yarn, raw hides and pelts, chemicals
(mainly sulphates of ammonia), rubber, tin and copper [139:
52–76]. These semi-manufactured goods were supplied chiefly
to other industrialising countries, as were exports of home-
produced raw materials, principally coal, some metal ores and
wool.

It was the relatively small re-export trade which increased most rapidly in this period, both in terms of volume and value, dominated by raw cotton, raw wool and raw silk. From about 11 per cent of import values in the 1850s, re-exports reached 19 per cent during the American Civil War, declining to 16 per cent for the following decade [15:*169–70*]. As a percentage of total exports the figure rose from about 16 per cent in the 1850s, rising to 24 per cent in the early 1860s, falling to 20 per cent between 1865 and 1875. Both exports and imports grew rapidly by more than 4 per cent per annum (national income rose by slightly less than 3 per cent per annum), but between the 1840s and the 1870s the relative importance of raw-material imports declined, due to the striking growth in the import of food-stuffs, especially grains and milled products, rice, vegetables and fruit, butter, cheese and eggs [139:*54–9*]. This trend is attributable to the effects of population growth, some improvement in living standards, and to the commercial policy of free trade. Free trade was also accompanied by an increase in the quantity of imported finished goods beginning in 1860. Before that date manufactured goods had been only an insignificant part of Britain's total imports and had, indeed, been re-exported to an increasing extent. Before 1865 the value of net imports of finished manufactured goods was less than 5 per cent of total imports for each quinquennium from 1833 to 1837, this percentage rose to 6·9 per cent for 1853–9, 10·6 per cent for 1860–4 and 13 per cent for 1865–9. It is interesting to note that when the Report of the Royal Commission on the Depression of Trade and Industry drew attention to the impact of foreign competition in the 1880s net imports of finished manufactured goods were barely one percentage point above that level, at 14 per cent [139:*68*].

The trade statistics thus point to an expansion of foreign trade which provided a major impetus to overall economic growth, and at least in the 1850s, produced an export-led boom of huge dimensions; even in the 1860s the rate of trade expansion continued to exceed that of the growth of national income. Market conditions, the result of actions both at home and abroad, provided the key to greater success in foreign trade, and steam transport was the major influence, as the railway networks of

Britain, Europe, the United States and India were vastly extended [1:*14–17*]. The iron steamship became a practical proposition for long-distance ocean cargo traffic when the compound engine was introduced in the 1860s, though its effective impact was not immediate. This made possible the large-scale movement of goods, a reduction in distribution costs, and the opening of new potential markets. Investment in transport was related to the internal industrialisation process in Europe and the United States, which in turn generated demands from Britain for a few consumer necessities and capital equipment. Product improvements and better productive techniques, especially in woollens, iron and steel and engineering, enhanced the economic opportunities presented by larger markets and cheaper distribution.

(i) FREE TRADE AND COMMERCIAL EXPANSION

It is not surprising that many contemporaries attributed the phenomenal expansion of international trade between the 1840s and 1880s to the implementation of free-trade policies, and especially vocal in this interpretation were those economists who had long campaigned in favour of free trade. James Wilson, founder and editor of *The Economist*, and Leone Levi in his *History of British Commerce and of Economic Progress of the British Nation 1763–1870* (1872), were among them. Historians have also been tempted to include free trade at the head of any list of factors which contributed to the expansion of the period, and Imlah's important study, *Economic Elements in the Pax Britannica* [15], proceeds to a climax in his final chapter entitled 'The Success of Free Trade Policy', following the chapter called 'The Failure of Protection'. More recently, Mathias stressed the crucial stimulus which free trade provided, resulting in an 'immense leap' in foreign-trade values, this great trading boom continuing until 1875. The mechanism was that of increased export markets following expanded imports into Britain which free trade now permitted [107:*302–3, 306*].

Just how important was free-trade policy? Between 1840 and 1860 the number of dutiable articles was reduced from more than 1100 in 1840, to barely 50 by 1860. Prior to 1845 the only imported finished manufacture that yielded an appreciable customs revenue was silk, and the removal of protection did not have very much effect on imports of other manufactures, for the obvious reason that the protection they enjoyed was largely unnecessary. In the eyes of contemporary free traders it was the duties on foodstuffs that mattered, and on corn in particular. For while the Corn Laws were symbolic in contemporary free-trade debates, corn was also practically the only important commodity which was predicted to be likely to experience a substantial rise in imports if free entry were allowed, assuming a high price elasticity for other imports subject to revenue duties. The overwhelming proportion of imports in the expansion between 1846 and 1873 were foodstuffs and raw materials, and a main plank in free traders' arguments had been that cheap food, following repeal, would expand the domestic market for manufactured goods, as well as increasing purchasing power in food-exporting countries. While it is arguable that with continued population growth grain prices might have been higher in the absence of repeal, the actual expansion in the domestic demand for manufactured goods could not have risen much by this particular mechanism, for wheat prices moved only marginally downwards, while barley and oats rose slightly. Tight and temporarily worsening grain supplies in Europe, which characterised the twenty years after repeal, help to explain the buoyancy of British cereal prices, added to which the flood of imports from the United States and Russia awaited the railways [9:*106–8*]. If we adopt the usual assumption that the demand for cereals was relatively price inelastic, total expenditure on non-food items is unlikely to have increased as a result of Corn Law repeal. Free trade did not herald an era of cheap food in the mid-Victorian years, and to that extent did not provide the major domestic stimulus to manufacturing industry which its champions had forecast.

Yet this does not imply that repeal was unimportant, for without it cereal prices might have risen steeply, curtailing domestic consumption of non-food products, and it is due to this eventuality that repeal is seen to have been important. The potential scarcity was relieved by substantial wheat imports which increased from 7·4 per cent as a percentage of estimated total consumption in England and Wales between 1829 and 1846; this figure rose to 26·6 per cent between 1849 and 1859, and to 40·1 per cent between 1860 and 1868 [9:*106–8*]. This growth in wheat imports raises an alternative possibility that repeal may have stimulated British exports via the foreign-trade multiplier. By this mechanism increased imports of cereals would have augmented incomes of exporters, enabling them to purchase additional British goods and services. The three major suppliers after 1846 were Russia, Prussia and the United States. Between 1845–9 and 1870–4 Russian wheat exports to the United Kingdom rose steadily from an annual average of 0·7 million cwt to 11·8 million cwt; comparable figures for Prussia are 3·1 million cwt in 1845–9, reaching a peak of about 5 million in 1860–4. Wheat exports from the United States to the United Kingdom grew erratically, but in 1860–4 reached 10 million cwt, fell off post-war, then exceeded the two rival suppliers in 1870–4 when the figure was 15 million cwt [112:*100–1*].

Despite these indications of enlarged purchasing power deriving specifically from cereal exports to the United Kingdom it would not be appropriate to proceed to the simple conclusion that the stimulating effect of Russian and Prussian demand resulting from this trade was of exceptional importance for British industry, for British exports to these countries hardly altered as a proportion of total British exports, except for the eventual fillip to Russian exports in the early 1870s. There is thus some reason to remain sceptical as far as bilateral trade is concerned, though it is possible that multilateral trading activity brought substantial gains to Britain indirectly [136:*44*], and is a question needing research.

While Corn Law repeal remains the most debated of the free-trade measures, this was one of several, with the Cobden–Chevalier Treaty signed by Britain and France in 1860 forming the culmination of negotiations towards free trade. Beginning in the quinquennium 1841–5, which marked the introduction of Peel's free-trade budget, and 1871–5, net imports rose from an annual average of £71 million to £302 million. At the same time, exports increased only slightly less rapidly, from £54 million to £240 million. Thus, foreign goods did not inundate the British market when her tariff barrier was removed. Indeed, the balance of merchandise trade improved [15:*165–6*], and imports took on a dependent quality, tending to be pulled up in the wake of a rise in the export of British goods and services. In this period when the sheer weight of foreign trade in the sum total of British activity was setting the pace for economic growth [56:*311–12*], the leading role of exports has been confirmed by Hughes for the 1850s, and for the 1860s (though to a lesser extent) and the early 1870s by Chaudhuri [43]. This is important, for it throws further doubt on the contention that the great Victorian trading boom was mainly due to free trade.

A surge in British exports was the immediate consequence of the Cobden–Chevalier Treaty, justifying the predictions of contemporary free traders. But the rapid rate of increase tapered off within two or three years, as French industrialists responded in positive fashion to the challenge of competition [134:*308–11*]. Whereas in the 1840s and early 1850s slightly fewer than 4 per cent of British exports were sold in France, even in the boom of the early 1870s this figure had risen to barely 7 per cent; and while the gradual reduction of import duties may have had some effect on Anglo-French trade, the trend of French imports and exports did not alter markedly between the 1820s and the 1870s [102:*749–97*]. This warns us against exaggerating the significance for British economic expansion of the Anglo-French Treaty, for there is some evidence to suggest that tariff reductions may not have been the autonomous factor in French economic growth and trade in the 1850s and 1860s [96:*304*]. Neither should we overstate the effects of the most-favoured-nation clauses incorporated in the Treaty which prevented discrimination against British exports. For it was not until 1865 that Germany, Belgium and Italy became part of the free-trade area. Meanwhile, in the United States the Tariff Act of 1846 reduced a number of duties on imported items, though many manufactured goods were protected by duties of 25 per cent and 30 per cent. A maximum duty of 24 per cent was agreed upon in 1857, but only four years later the Morrill Tariff marked an end to the relative free trade of the 1850s and a return to high levels of protection, followed by further restrictive measures in 1864 [128:279].

The general consensus among historians is that free trade played little part in American economic growth in this period [55:322]. Engerman has shown that the course of British iron exports to the United States were influenced more by the changing price of British iron than by tariff levels [59:23–4]. Russian earnings, derived from substantial wheat exports to Britain, were insufficient, due to internal financial burdens in a low-income society [62:419–20], to generate a strong reciprocal demand for British exports, while tariffs also remained high. Added to these difficulties the American Civil War and the Austro-Prussian War disrupted commercial intercourse and offset the gains which might have been expected from the free-trade agreements. Again, as with exports and net imports, it may be misleading to attribute a major role to commercial policy in the very rapid rate of growth of re-exports, which is a special feature of intra-European trade in this period. Before the 1860s these consisted mainly of colonial wares, and their level as a percentage of general imports fluctuated from the 1820s between 10 and 13 per cent. Then came a rise in the late 1850s reaching 17·5 per cent in the 1860s, but this was associated mainly with the growing demand for wool and cotton by continental textile manufacturers, together with the effects of the Cotton Famine. Britain's important role as a distributing centre for overseas commodities was a product of her historical development as a maritime colonial, commercial and industrial power, and it is not surprising that when industrialisation was proceeding on the Continent, Britain should have been able to supply many commodities efficiently at relatively low cost.

There seems to be insufficient evidence to vindicate those contemporary free traders who predicted that the growth in imports would generate higher export levels (which Imlah and Mathias have also argued was the case) and would check the export of British capital [16:127]. The reduction of British tariff barriers did not result in a flooding of British markets by foreign goods, but neither did British goods flood Europe, the region most involved in the new free-trading system. Trade with Europe grew steadily between the booms of the early 1850s (when Europe's share fell temporarily) and the boom of the

63

(when Europe's share was unusually high) [139: ... while her share of British exports remained relatively ... levels between 33 and 38 per cent (see Table 5).

Table 5

Percentage Distribution of U.K. Exports by Continents, 1850–74 (values)

Years	Europe	North America	Central and S. America	Asia	Levant
1850–4	29·8	26·6	9·6	13·0	4·2
1855–9	33·3	19·5	9·1	16·5	6·0
1860–4	33·2	14·3	9·4	18·5	6·5
1865–9	38·2	20·9	9·9	18·4	8·0
1870–4	40·1	17·7	9·3	15·2	5·8

SOURCE: [113:*315–21*]

An additional reason for retaining a cautious view of the impact of free trade on British industry lies in the commodity composition of British trade with the two largest markets, Europe and the United States, which began to reflect a shift towards the export of raw materials, especially coal, semi-manufactured goods, iron and steel, and machinery, the inputs for industrialisation. To these were added the export of textile yarns to the Continent, where manufacturers of woollen and cotton textiles piece goods were mechanising for competition with British manufacturers. Whereas in 1840 Europe and the United States took nearly 30 per cent of British exports of cotton piece goods, this figure fell to 19 per cent in 1860 and to barely 12 per cent in 1870 [58:*64*]. Within Europe, the rising trend in exports to the non-industrial countries contrasted with a relative decline in exports to the industrial regions [139:*81–6*]. As European and American manufacturers were successful in supplying an increasing share of their domestic markets, the trade in cotton and wool textiles became increasingly a trade based on complementarity in terms of quality and finish. Offsetting these tendencies was the growth of trade with Asia and the Middle East, due in part to the Crimean and Opium wars, and the search for alternative supplies of cotton, especially during the American Civil War. Both developments led to British expenditure in these areas, which was followed by a sharp rise in British exports of consumer goods, mainly cotton piece goods, to India, China, Turkey and to a lesser extent, Egypt. Adding to this upward surge of trade with primary-producing countries, the income effects of the Australian gold discoveries temporarily raised the importance of that country as a market for textiles and hardware [12:40].

For a very long time the strong free-trade hypothesis has remained unchallenged. Yet, although the theoretical basis of the argument is forceful, historians have neglected to establish whether the facts fit the theory. The unprecedented absolute increase in the volume of international trade between 1842 and 1873 is undeniable, but it is also true that the rate of growth in the volume of trade during these years followed the upward trend of preceding decades.[14] Furthermore, Imlah's study [15] concentrated upon the movement of aggregate figures, rather than exploring specific types of trade and the influence of specific tariff concessions. Before we are able to assess with confidence the effects of commercial policies on the magnitudes and patterns of trade in this period, it will be necessary to formulate explicitly models outlining the modes and mechanisms by which specific commodities might have been effected. This will require detailed examination of changes in those factors, other than price, which may have influenced the demand for commodities directly affected by tariff reductions – prices of substitutes, consumers' incomes and preferences. Similarly there will need to be a more detailed consideration of international trading patterns in order to elucidate the extent to which, and the processes by which, reductions in duties affected the volume of trade, both in goods and services. In the present state of research all we can say is that on the basis of empirical evidence a positive judgement seems to be unwarranted.

(ii) CAPITAL EXPORTS

Although after its initial impact on bilateral European commerce the direct effects of free trade might not perhaps have been very great, the growth in Britain's re-export trade with some European countries suggests that European free trade may have raised the level of international trade through multilateral trading links with other regions and so helps to explain the rapid trade expansion between Britain and the underdeveloped countries. The difficulties of establishing a viable trading sector for such countries in normal conditions, however, were enormous, their effective purchasing power being hampered by low incomes and dependent, to a considerable extent, upon their ability to borrow. These were totally different circumstances from those of the developed economies in Europe, where markets were relatively stable and wealthy, dependent not upon British credit and means of payment but on income generated mainly within those countries. Of critical importance to the underdeveloped economies were the prices of primary products they supplied in relation to the prices of manufactured goods they purchased. Before the 1850s export prices had declined faster than the prices of imported commodities and boosted British exports. From the mid-1850s to the mid-1860s the net barter terms of trade moved indecisively, followed by a definitely favourable shift during the 1870s export boom in British capital goods, iron and coal, whose prices rose sharply under pressure of demand [15:*102*]. The terms of trade, therefore, cannot have enhanced the ability of primary producers to purchase manufactured goods from Britain in the third quarter of the century.

Borrowing was the remaining solution which could transform a willingness to purchase into effective demand. For Asian and African countries, trade credit extended by British merchants with the accompanying transfer of sterling balances was an important determinant of the level of British exports, as it had been also to countries outside Europe and the United States in the early years of the century [108:*77–8*]. But trade credit was only one form of borrowing available to other countries, and the mid-1850s saw the beginnings of substantial and diverse forms of foreign investment in the underdeveloped economies. Before 1850, capital accumulated abroad had proceeded slowly to reach just over £200 million, on which British investors received annual interest of £11·7 million. Between 1856 and 1875 capital exports ran at an annual rate of

£75 million, perhaps increasing faster than domestic investment, and whereas in the earlier period income from abroad in interest and dividends usually exceeded new foreign lending, in the mid-Victorian period capital outflows exceeded the accruing interest available for re-investment.

Furthermore, the new capital exports differed in kind and in direction. In 1850 about two-thirds of British-held foreign assets originated in Europe and mainly took the form of loan stock of various north European governments and a much lesser part in the form of private direct investment and trade credit. The remaining British foreign investment, approximately one-third, was in America. In the third quarter of the century Europe and the United States continued to be recipients of sizeable British capital investments in the form mainly of railway stocks carrying a guaranteed government dividend; or in greater quantities of fixed interest securities issued by governments (national, provincial and municipal), themselves undertaking the construction of railway systems and other public utilities. The flow to America, however, was checked temporarily during the Civil War years. Outside Europe, Turkey borrowed substantial amounts, having been brought into the ambit of European finance as a result of military activities in the Crimea. Russia, Peru and Egypt also figured in British foreign investments towards the end of the period.

In the absence of very reliable estimates before 1865 it is difficult to assess the magnitude and distribution of foreign investment with accuracy, but Habakkuk has estimated that the proportion of new capital investment abroad suggests that between 1850 and 1875 at least two-fifths of the *increase* in the amount of capital invested abroad went to the Empire [10: *788*]. Simon's estimates for 1865 to 1869 show that the figure was 40 per cent, but this fell to less than 20 per cent during the great boom in Europe between 1870 and 1874 [145: *Table II*]. Increasing overseas investment was, in part, the corollary o Britain's success as an invisible exporter. Thanks to the earnings of British shipping, from interest, dividends and profit on foreign trade, and income from insurance, brokerage and commissions, Britain's mounting balance-of-trade deficit was turned into an overall balance-of-payments surplus. Capital exports to the Empire thus generated effective demand for goods and services in the receiving countries, and without this mechanism the Empire's share in British markets would have been much lower. This was especially important from the standpoint of Anglo-Imperial trade. The historical and institutional links established between Britain and the colonies ensured that from the 1850s, when the movement of capital became the primary economic relationship between the United Kingdom and the colonies, her administrative abilities were in demand. Britain had to supply not only the original capital but the initial direction, whether it was in public-works construction, railway enterprise, banking or tea cultivation: 'the Empire became, in a new sense, an integral part of the British economic system' [10: *798*]. One result of this connection was that, whereas only a small proportion of British loans to foreign governments was spent directly on British rails and engines, a large part of colonial loans was spent on railways, canals, irrigation works, and spent fairly directly on British goods, specifically upon products of the iron and metal industries.

How is the growth in capital exports in the mid-nineteenth century to be explained? J. A Hobson and various Marxist writers have argued, mainly for a later period, that the pressure to export surplus capital arising within a developed capitalist economy was the principal force generating overseas expansion of the Empire, which in turn led to a redirection of capital towards newly acquired territories. But in our period in the case of Australia, the gold discoveries and the consequent internal developments provided the motive for capital export, while in India the strategic necessities of improved communication which the Mutiny had demonstrated, added to the wish to develop that country as a supplier of raw cotton, lay behind the heavy investment there in transport and utilities [105]. To India, to Europe, to North and South America, British capital was exported in connection with railway development. The readiness of British investors to finance overseas railways in this period contrasted with difficulties encountered by British railway companies in attracting investment. In part this reflected the stage reached by the domestic railway system in which the most profitable lines had been built already; but other factors, highly geared financial structures, and the prohibition since 1847 of the payment of interest on calls, provided further explanation for the relative disinterest in British railway investment by the public in the 1850s and early 1860s [127: *43–4*]. Cairncross has argued that where British investors preferred foreign and colonial securities, it was because they could expect a marginally higher rate of return than from comparable British assets, and while the scanty comparative data available relates mainly to the 1870s and after, he implies that this interpretation holds for the sixty years before 1914 [39: *228–32*].

Until it becomes possible to conduct a detailed and systematic comparison of the yields of British, foreign and colonial securities, it seems desirable to maintain at least a sceptical view of the notion that there existed in Britain at this time a surplus of capital which *had* to be exported to earn positive rates of return. Rates of interest do not appear to have fallen during the twenty years following the commercial crisis of 1847, and there was a widening in the outlets for joint-stock investment in this period of rapid industrial expansion. Furthermore, net foreign investment rose simultaneously with gross fixed-domestic-capital formation, which suggests that circumstances which were favourable to investment at home also stimulated investment overseas. The revolution in transport and British and European migration, in particular to North America, stimulated British capital exports to finance European, American and Indian railways. A by-product of the opening up of land, especially in the areas of recent settlement, was urban concentration at the ports and nodal transport centres which required further capital imports for development [77: *3*]. Railways were at the centre of the secular boom in British foreign investment in this period, though some capital exports, notably to Turkey, were also due to the Crimean War. The income effects of investment in overseas railways were felt strongly at home, and the synchronisation of home and overseas railway development acted as a powerful lever on the rate of economic growth.

Both trade and capital exports were instrumental in the achievement of maximum rates of economic growth in the mid-nineteenth century. The precise contribution of a shift in commercial policy to free trade is at least uncertain and probably exaggerated in the conventional interpretation, but the expansion of trade with recipients of British capital testifies to the importance of the mechanism linking capital exports with trade. Moreover, the explanation for capital movements, partly as a positive response to relatively attractive opportunities overseas and partly to speculation, is indicative of the essential dynamism of mid-Victorian capitalism.

5 Mid-Victorian Prosperity

THE years between 1850 and 1873 are often described as an era of mid-Victorian prosperity. Although contemporary economists were not unanimous in their assessment, the optimistic view seems to have predominated – an interpretation which continues to receive wide support in some popular texts.[15] Feinstein's estimates of real national income show a rise between 1855 and 1873 by 46 per cent, most of which occurred in the boom of the 1870s. Contrary to what might be expected, estimates of real wages of artisans, constructed by Tucker and Phelps Brown and Hopkins, suggest that *per capita* incomes rose at roughly similar rates in the third and second quarters of the century[16] – the latter period often characterised as one of depression, discontent and social tension, with which it has become customary for historians to contrast the socio-political stability of the mid-Victorian 'age of equipoise', when economic prosperity was the palliative [98:*47*; 157:*279*; 81:*269*]. The income statistics with which historians must work are, if anything, even less satisfactory than those relating to investment and production, but the general impression derived from the most recent assessments is that the Victorians prospered more in the 1860s than in the 1850s and that there was at the same time a more than proportionate increase in the number and incomes of the middle income group [3; 119; 27]. Wage-earners probably fared less well than the middle-income groups, including those who mounted the social ladder in this period.

When unemployment, which exaggerated the rise in incomes before the 1870s, is taken into account, the increase in average real wages between 1850 and 1873 was less than 33 per cent [126:*215–16*], and only from the mid-sixties does a discontinuous, but nevertheless marked, upward trend become unmistakable (see Table 6, p. 72). Within the wage-earning group,

71

skilled workers gained most, notably cotton and building workers, and to a lesser extent engineers, shipbuilders and printers, while the differential in earnings between unskilled and skilled workers may well have increased due to cyclical unemployment. Serious deficiencies in employment figures for the nineteenth century make it extremely difficult to offer more than an impressionistic picture of unemployment, even among unionised labour, between 1851 and 1873. Coppock's figures, which relate only to engineering, metal manufacture and ship-building, show an average of 5 per cent unemployment among union labour compared with 7·2 per cent between 1874 and 1895 during the so-called Great Depression [52:*394*]. When,

Table 6

G. H. Wood's Index of Real Wages. U.K. 1850=100

1850—100	1855— 94	1860—105	1865—120	1870—118
1851—102	1856— 95	1861— 99	1866—117	1871—125
1852—100	1857— 94	1862—100	1867—105	1872—126
1853—107	1858— 94	1863—107	1868—105	1873—132
1854— 97	1859—104	1864—118	1869—111	1874—136

NOTE: Allowance is made for unemployment. 1850 is mid-way between the cyclical trough of 1847 and the peak of 1853.

SOURCE: [160].

for the purposes of greater comparability in the movements of economic variables, the period is extended from 1874 to 1899, the figure is 6·7 per cent as compared with 5 per cent in the preceding period. When all trade unions are included (which probably covered fewer than 5 per cent of the occupied labour force at this time) the figures for the two periods are 4·5 per cent (1851–73) and 5 per cent (1874–99) [120]. This suggests that average unemployment levels may not have differed substantially in the mid-Victorian boom and the late Victorian 'depression'. This is not very surprising when the trade-union returns show that the depression of 1858 saw 11·9 per cent of members out of work, a larger percentage than in 1879 or 1886; for 1862 the figure was 8·4 per cent, and for 1868, 7·9 per cent. These rough indicators provide further justification for stressing the elements of instability in the mid-Victorian economic expansion.

The figures disclosing unemployment and stagnating real wages for most of the period also suggest that we should not conclude that because there was a tightening of seasonal labour supplies in the agricultural sector [90], urban industrial labour also became relatively scarcer in the mid-nineteenth century. Where technical innovation was proceeding rapidly, the displacement of handicraft labour was still often a corollary,[17] furthermore in those industries as yet unaffected by mechanisation and factory organisation, extensive casual employment was an indication of an under-utilisation of labour resources, notably in agriculture and the outwork industries of London, the Black Country and the East Midlands [26; 46].[18] Even taking into account the continuation of an upward trend of real incomes into the 1890s, Best reckoned that the extent of poverty in the 1850s and 1860s was probably not very different from that discovered by Booth and Rowntree in the 1890s [3:*124*]. Indeed net emigration from England and Wales, at this time attributed by Thomas principally to 'push' factors, ran at levels less than one-fifth below the figures for the 1840s, actually representing a higher decennial rate [147:*124,Table 35*]. In terms of real income, mid-Victorian prosperity was limited, both in time and extent. It is to be found increasing only towards the end of the period, and even then largely among the middle classes and skilled operatives. Regional income differentials increased, with London, the industrial Northern counties and the Midlands as far south as Birmingham, retaining the lead, though local studies suggest that even in the Black Country and Merseyside there was no substantial rise in living stands until the end of our period [29:*103*]. Industrial expansion increased the demand for skilled and high-productivity labour located in industrial areas, and the result of this was to perpetuate regional variations in wages, producing what one historian has recently described as a 'dual economy', arguably rendering even more dubious the use of the general label 'mid-Victorian prosperity' [14:*181*]. Our knowledge of the extent of, and reasons for, these regional differences, must await further detailed research, but if the overall extent of unemployment and underemployment can be shown to have been relatively high, then this would go far to invalidate McCloskey's thesis that labour was the bottleneck which by 1870 was beginning to inhibit industrial growth [104].

It is not clear why incomes did not expand correspondingly until the 1860s, despite the rapid rate of growth. The contemporary economist, William Newmarch, suggested that railway building involved the diversion of such a quantity of resources for investment distant in time from final output that consumption had to be compressed [150: *367–71*]. He was referring in particular to railway investment, to which in the 1850s was added a higher level of government expenditure associated with the Crimean War, and higher levels, relative to preceding decades, of foreign investment. In Rostovian terminology each of these categories of expenditure was of lengthy gestation, and thus contributed little to the raising of real income in the short run. But this analysis implies an enormously and improbably long gestation period before investment resulted in rising *per capita* incomes, and it also implies a level of capital formation exceeding by far the best estimates available to us. Population growth, another influence on *per capita* incomes, was affected by net emigration in the 1850s, which meant that the net addition to population in the 1850s was slightly smaller than that which occurred in the 1860s. Even so, *per capita* incomes in the 1850s rose barely perceptibly at a time when industrial productivity, if we are to believe Hoffman's figures, was at its peak. When in the 1860s industrial productivity began to falter, *per capita* real incomes began to rise. A possible explanation for this seemingly perverse relationship in the 1860s may be found in the changing economic structure, with an increase in the relative importance of transport and trade, where productivity may have been higher; added to which from the late 1850s the terms of trade may have moved slightly in Britain's favour, with a markedly favourable shift from 1868 to 1873.

For whatever reasons, the course of real wages for the mass of the population does not appear to have risen substantially before the mid-1860s, and to portray this as an era of mid-Victorian social tranquillity [39: *17*; 3: *228*] when prosperity was the anodyne [98: *47*] ignores both the chronology and trend in real wages. G. D. H. Cole concluded, long ago, that neither the 1850s nor the 1860s brought industrial peace, while 'the late 1860s and early 1870s were in fact a period of very considerable trade union militancy'.[19] In this counterpoint of prosperity and industrial conflict, prosperity acted as a stimulant rather than as a bromide.

6 Conclusion

ARE historians justified in referring to the period between 1850 and 1873, or thereabouts, as the Great Victorian Boom? Our answer is a severely qualified affirmative. Because prices rose spectacularly for a time, because the secular rate of economic growth achieved its nineteenth-century maximum, because business expansion and speculation did occur and living standards eventually improved significantly, the labels Great Victorian Boom and Mid-Victorian Prosperity contain sufficient truth to conceal their several defects; but continued employment of these terms encourages distortion in historical perspective and invites error in interpretation. The difference between the rate of growth in immediately preceding decades and in the comparable time period after 1873 was relatively small, which hardly justifies attributing to 1850–73 a special unity. While economic growth was very significant in this period as a whole it must have been extraordinarily great at times, in 1853–6, 1863–5 and 1871–3, as it seems to have been very limited at others. What was possibly the most profound depression of the century occurred in 1858. The period was not, as the author of a recent textbook would have it, the time when 'spasmodic growth gave way to regular and rapid growth'[20]; mid-Victorian growth was a product of instability to which, from the beginning, the railways' contribution was very important, though less than critical. Between the inflations of 1853–5 and 1870–2 the most striking characteristic of price trends was a relative stability at high levels, with a mildly deflationary trend setting in after the American Civil War. We should be sceptical of historians who juxtapose rising prices and economic growth, as if in partial explanation of each other, for although rapid growth in the 1850s coincided with rising prices, the maximum growth rates appear to have been sustained from

1858, during a period of relative price stability, until the cyclical inflationary boom of the early 1870s.

Neither in terms of prices nor growth does the period possess a distinctive unity. Different sectors experienced differing price trends and disparate intrasectoral price-movements affected patterns of profitability and investment. In agriculture such a process explained the basis of mid-Victorian prosperity, uneven though it was as between different types of farming and between receivers of profits, rents and wages. The movement of intrasectoral prices, of inputs and outputs, produced disparities within the industrial sector, too, and we have suggested that it may be misleading to assume that although profits grew this was also a period of profit inflation, easy gain and entrepreneurial euphoria. In the largest industrial sector – textiles – changing price and cost relationships, reinforced by intense competition, stimulated the adoption of innovation and investment, expansion of capacity and output. The current debate on investment and the diffusion of technology has focused almost exclusively upon the effects of changes in demand, or wages, or the price of capital, upon profitability. Our cursory review of the evidence suggests that both because of their relative importance in cost structures and their volatility, movements in raw-material prices deserve comparable attention if we are seeking to enhance our understanding of the basis and character of mid-Victorian business expansion. The artificial stimulus of war demands produced a similar process of discontinuous development in iron, steel, shipbuilding and coal, with alternating periods, in all sectors, of high and low levels of output employment and profits. Investment and technological change also led to industrial relocation, accompanied by intrasectoral decline in certain regions and industries. Such a complex situation was hardly conducive, except perhaps for the redoubtable and peculiarly insensitive Samuel Smiles, to general entrepreneurial complacency, notwithstanding British industrial pre-eminence. Competition from a domestic producer was equally threatening to a firm's profits and survival as competition from overseas, and it is only at the level of individual enterprise, which forms the fulcrum of investment, that notions of euphoria have any meaning. Furthermore, even before the 1860s, weaknesses

77

were being exposed and publicised, heralding the inevitable intensification of competition with the emerging industrial countries.

Industrialisation outside Britain was assisted by British capital exports, and these, like capital exports to the primary-producing countries and to the Middle East, generated overseas demand for British goods. This mechanism contributed significantly to the enormous mid-Victorian trading expansion, but whether British free-trade policy was in a very large measure responsible for the trading boom is, in the present state of research, doubtful. It is clear, however, that free trade meant that prices of some basic foodstuffs were lower than they would have been otherwise, but rising real wages and the relative prosperity often associated with this period was limited in extent, and only became marked from the mid-1860s. Meanwhile, shifts in the trend of prices, interest rates, net manufactured imports and industrial productivity, together signify that in many respects the mid-1860s may be interpreted as forming an important economic watershed, the commercial crisis of 1866 and the reactions to it bringing to an end that cyclical dynamism so characteristic of mid-Victorian industrial capitalism and arguably essential to unprecedented levels of economic growth. The 1860s emerge as a decade in need of research.

We suggest that an understanding of these years would be enhanced if historians were to concentrate less on national macroeconomic aggregates and more on microeconomic, regional developments; to focus less on the Great Victorian Boom, and pay more attention, as did contemporary businessmen, to the great Victorian investment booms of 1852–3, 1863–5 and 1871–3. The salient economic features of the period include spells of rising, falling and stable prices; uncertainty as well as speculation and optimism; pressures on profit margins as well as windfall gains; checks to output and idle resources, competition, expansion and high levels of employment; stagnant and rapidly rising real wages. By the criterion of the nineteenth century the mid-Victorian years experienced marked, but relatively unspectacular, economic growth; in most other respects – notably price trends, euphoria and prosperity – the conception of a distinctive historical unity for 1850–73 is a myth.

Notes and References

1. The theoretical solution was provided by J. R. Hicks, *A Contribution to the Theory of the Trade Cycle* (Oxford, 1950) p. 154, n. 1.

2. The aggregate of bills and bank deposits always exceeded banknotes in circulation and bankers' gold reserves [12:236]. At their peak, between 1860 and 1870, inland bills averaged 83 per cent of National Income [22:*Table 18*].

3. Note W. A. Cole's critical appraisal of Hoffman's indices and his conclusion that 'likelihood of error before 1830 and after 1870 seems greater than in the intervening decades', in 'The Measurement of Industrial Growth', *Economic History Review*, 2nd ser., xi (1958) p. 314.

4. Britain's annual average rate of growth of 2 per cent for 1858–75 compares with a 'slow grower' French peak rate of 3 per cent for 1847–59 [121:*53*].

5. Deane's estimates of annual rates of growth in the G.N.P. for the United Kingdom are (in percentages): 1·7 for 1840–50; 2·5 for 1850–60; and 2·6 for 1860–70. For Britain the decadal differences would be diminished by the elimination of the low Irish growth rate in the 1840s [8].

6. Gross expenditure on railway capital as a percentage of Deane's revised estimates of Fixed Domestic Capital Formation.

1850–4	24·3	1865–9	21·7
1855–9	21·3	1870–4	14·6
1860–4	24·5		

The figures for the 1850s are from Mitchell [112], the remainder from Hawke [11].

7. Feinstein's figures for net domestic-capital formation as a percentage of net domestic product in 1855–74 and 1875–94 are 7·0 per cent and 6·8 per cent respectively [64].

8. A breakdown of costs in the cotton industry by Ellison shows the following distribution.

	Cost of Cotton (per cent)	Wages (per cent)	Other Expenses* (per cent)
1829–31	20·9	36·2	42·9
1844–6	25·6	31·3	43·1
1859–61	36·5	25·8	37·7
1880–2	36·0	27·4	36·6

SOURCE: [58:*69*].

The cost structure of the Ashworth enterprise in the 1840s shows that excluding capital costs raw materials accounted for 70 per cent in the production of yarn and 68 per cent in cloth manufacture. For worsted the Black Dyke Mills figures in the 1840s also indicate raw-material costs of at least 70 per cent [144:*242–3*; 34:*48*].

* Including dyes, fuel, maintenance, depreciation, interest on capital, profits, etc.

9. Raw-material costs of Greenwood & Batley's machine-tool firm in the second half of the century was 16 per cent of total costs [69: *330*]. In the manufacture of soap, Crosfield's raw-material costs accounted for 60 per cent of total costs [116:*91–4*].

10. *Select Committee on the Causes of the Present Dearness and Scarcity of Coal* (1873, x), Report XI, evidence of Elliott, qu. 7625–30; evidence of Pease, qu. 4362–3.

11. The statistics on bankruptcy are virtually worthless for long-term analysis, though for cyclical indicators see Hoffman [82: *Table 54*]. Robert Giffen expressed the view that, regardless of the figures (which supported him), there had been a declining trend in bankruptcies since the early 1870s: *Royal Commission on the Depression of Trade and Industry* (1886, XXI), Table 42 and qu. 128–32.

12. It is interesting to note that of those businessmen asked in 1833 to declare what they considered to be 'reasonable' profits (distinct from actual realised earnings) in the 1830s, replies varied between 10 per cent and 16 per cent on capital. *Select Committee on Manufactures, Commerce and Shipping* 1833, VI, ev. of Lewis Lloyd (Manchester banker), qu. 592–3; ev. of Anthony Hill (Welsh Ironmaster), qu. 10399; ev. of Henry Nelson (London Shipowner), qu. 6521.

13. For an explicit statement, see [116:*91–4*] and [93:*383–5*].

14. Volume of exports and imports, compound rates of growth per cent per annum:

1801–31	2·6	1831–61	4·5
1811–41	4·0	1841–70	4·6
1821–51	4·4	1850–80	4·1

SOURCE: [56: *Table 83*].

15. For example, 'The Great Exhibition of 1851 ushered in an age of prosperity which lasted virtually until 1873', Pauline Gregg [75: *295*]. See also Asa Briggs, *The Age of Improvement* (1962) pp. 394, 402–4.

16. Perkin's table shows the figures for annual percentage rate of change in real wages as follows:

	Tucker	Brown and Hopkins
1815/19–1845/9	0·7	1·1
1845/9–1871/5	0·6	0·7
1871/5–1894/8	1·2	2·2

SOURCE: [120].

17. John Saville, *Rural Depopulation in England and Wales 1851–1957* (1957) pp. 26–7.

18. Henry Mayhew, in [109: *322*], may have been exaggerating when he claimed that one-third of the operatives of the entire country were in regular full-time employment, one-third in half-time (casual) employment, and the remainder unemployed; but in some areas the essential problem he raised was central to Victorian society [91; 29; 14].

19. G. D. H. Cole, 'Some Notes on British Trade Unionism in the Third Quarter of the Nineteenth Century', *International Review of Social History*, II (1937).

20. Richard Tames, *Economy and Society in Nineteenth-Century Britain* (1972) p. 21.

Select Bibliography

UNLIKE the 'Industrial Revolution' or the 'Great Depression', the 'Great Victorian Boom' has not been the subject of intense debate; the compilation of a select bibliography is thus extremely difficult, for much of what is relevant is often to be found as peripheral sections of books and articles principally concerned with other periods or problems. We have decided, therefore, to provide full references to the secondary sources we have used and to indicate, in section I, the more important books and articles which either focus mainly on the mid-Victorian years, or which contain substantial sections devoted to them. Unless otherwise indicated, London is the place of publication. The abbreviation *E.H.R.* represents *Economic History Review*.

SECTION I

[1] W. Ashworth, *An Economic History of England 1870–1939* (1960).

[2] H. L. Beales, 'The Great Depression in Industry and Trade', *E.H.R.*, v (1934).

[3] Geoffrey Best, *Mid-Victorian Britain* (1972).

[4] J. D. Chambers, *The Workshop of the World* (1961).

[5] S. G. Checkland, *The Rise of Industrial Society in England* (1964).

[6] J. H. Clapham, *An Economic History of Modern Britain*, vol. II (Cambridge, 1932).

[7] E. W. Cooney, 'Long Waves in Building in the British Economy of the Nineteenth Century', *E.H.R.*, 2nd ser., XIII (1960).

[8] Phyllis Deane, 'New Estimates of Gross National Product for the United Kingdom 1830–1914', *Review of Income and Wealth*, XIV (1968).

[9] Susan Fairlie, 'The Corn Laws and British Wheat Production 1829–1876', *E.H.R.*, 2nd ser., XXII (1969).

[10] H. J. Habakkuk, 'Free Trade and Commercial Expansion of the British Empire', in *The Cambridge History of the British Empire*, vol. II (1940).

[11] G. R. Hawke, *Railways and Economic Growth in England and Wales 1840–1870* (Oxford, 1970).

[12] J. R. T. Hughes, *Fluctuations in Trade, Industry and Finance 1850–1860* (Oxford, 1960).

[13] ——, 'Wickwell on the Facts: Prices and Interest Rates 1844–1914', in *Value, Capital and Growth*, ed. J. N. Wolfe (Edinburgh, 1968).

[14] E. H. Hunt, *Regional Wage Variations in Wages in England and Wales 1850–1914* (1973).

[15] A. Imlah, *Economic Elements in the Pax Britannica* (Harvard, 1958).

[16] L. H. Jenks, *The Migration of British Capital to 1875* (1927).

[17] E. L. Jones, *The Development of English Agriculture 1815–1873* (1968).

[18] D. S. Landes, 'Technological Change and Development in Western Europe 1750–1914', in *Cambridge Economic History of Europe*, vol. VI, part 1 (Cambridge, 1965).

[19] W. T. Layton and G. Crowther, *An Introduction to the Study of Prices* (1935).

[20] Parry Lewis, *Building Cycles and British Growth* (1965).

[21] R. C. O. Mathews, *The Trade Cycle* (Cambridge, 1959).

[22] Shizuya Nishimura, *The Decline of Inland Bills of Exchange in the London Money Market 1855–1913* (Cambridge, 1971).

[23] W. W. Rostow, *The British Economy of the 19th Century* (Oxford, 1948).

[24] J. Saville, 'Comments on Professor Rostow's British Economy of the 19th Century', *Past and Present* (1954).

SECTION II

[25] D. H. Aldcroft and P. Fearon (eds) *British Economic Fluctuations 1790–1939* (1972).

[26] G. C. Allen, *The Industrial Development of Birmingham and the Black Country* (1929).

[27] J. A. Banks, *Prosperity and Parenthood* (1954).

[28] T. C. Barker, *Pilkingtons and the Glass Industry* (1960).

[29] G. J. Barnsby, 'The Standard of Living in the Black Country in the Nineteenth Century', *E.H.R.*, 2nd ser., XXIV (1971).

[30] R. Dudley Baxter, 'Railway Extension and Its Results', in *Essays in Economic History*, vol. iii, ed. E. M. Carus Wilson (1962).

[31] J. R. Bellerby, 'National Income and Agricultural Income 1851', *Economic Journal*, LXIX (1957).

[32] Alan Birch, *The Economic History of the British Iron and Steel Industry, 1784–1879* (1967).

[33] M. Blaug, 'The Productivity of Capital in the Lancashire Cotton Industry during the Nineteenth Century', *E.H.R.*, 2nd ser., XIII (1961).

[34] Rhodes Boyson, *The Ashworth Cotton Enterprises* (1970).

[35] E. A. Brady, 'A Reconstruction of the Lancashire Cotton Famine', *Agricultural History*, XVI (1963).

[36] Keith Burgess, 'Technological Change and the 1852 Lock-out in the British Engineering Industry', *International Review of Social History*, XIV (1969).

[37] D. L. Burn, 'The Genesis of American Engineering Competition 1850–1870', *Economic History*, II (1931).

[38] ——, *The Economic History of Steelmaking 1867–1939* (Cambridge, 1961).

[39] A. Cairncross, *Home and Foreign Investment 1870–1913* (Cambridge, 1953).

[40] J. E. Cairnes, *Essays in Political Economy* (1873).

[41] Rondo Cameron, *Banking in the Early Stages of Industrialization* (Oxford, 1967).

[42] J. C. Carr and W. Taplin, *History of the British Steel Industry* (1962).

[43] P. H. Chaudhuri, 'Foreign Trade and Economic Growth: The Balance of Payments as a Factor Limiting Economic Expansion in the British Economy' (unpublished M.Sc. thesis, University of Cambridge, 1963).

[44] S. G. Checkland, 'Growth and Progress: The Nineteenth-Century View in Britain', *E.H.R.*, 2nd ser., XIII (1959/60).

[45] Jean Cheetham, 'Changes in the Pattern of the British Export Trades (with special reference to the Continent) between 1851 and 1873' (unpublished M.A.(Econ.) thesis, University of Manchester, 1955).

[46] R. A. Church, 'Labour Supply and Innovation: The Boot and Shoe Industry 1800–1860', *Business History*, XII, 1 (1970).

[47] ——, *Economic and Social Change in a Midland Town: Victorian Nottingham 1815–1900* (1966).

[48] D. C. Coleman, *The British Paper Industry 1495–1850* (1958).

[49] D. C. Coleman, *Courtaulds*, vol. I (1969).

[50] E. J. T. Collins and E. L. Jones, 'Sectoral Advance in English Agriculture, 1850–1880', *Agricultural History Review*, xv (1967).

[51] D. J. Coppock, 'The Climacteric of the 1890s: A Critical Note', *Manchester School*, xxiv (1956).

[52] ——, 'British Industrial Growth during the Great Depression 1873–1896: A Pessimist's View', *E.H.R.*, 2nd ser., xvii (1964).

[53] P. L. Cottrell, 'The Financial Sector and Economic Growth: England in the Nineteenth Century', *Istituto Italiano per la Storia dei Movimenti Sociali e delle Strutture Sociali*, 1 (1972).

[54] Paul David, 'Labour Productivity in English Agriculture 1850–1914: Some Quantitative Evidence on Regional Differences', *E.H.R.*, 2nd ser., xxviii (1970).

[55] Lance E. Davis, Jonathan R. T. Hughes and Duncan McDougall, *American Economic History* (Illinois, 1961).

[56] Phyllis Deane and W. A. Cole, *British Economic Growth 1688–1959* (Cambridge, 1969).

[57] H. J. Dyos, *Victorian Suburb: A Study of the Growth of Camberwell* (Leicester, 1961).

[58] Thomas Ellison, *The Cotton Trade of Great Britain* (1886).

[59] S. Engerman, 'The American Tariff, British Exports and American Iron Production 1840–1860', in *Essays on a Mature Economy: Britain after 1840*, ed. D. N. McCloskey (1972).

[60] Charlotte Erickson, *British Industrialists: Steel and Hosiery 1850–1950* (1959).

[61] Susan Fairlie, 'The Nineteenth Century Corn Law Reconsidered', *E.H.R.*, 2nd ser., xviii (1965).

[62] M. E. Falkus, 'Russia and the International Wheat Trade 1861–1914', *Economica*, new ser., xxxiii (1966).

[63] D. A. Farnie, 'The English Cotton Industry 1850–1896 (unpublished M.A. thesis, University of Manchester, 1953).

[64] C. H. Feinstein, *National Income, Expenditure and Output of the United Kingdom 1855–1965* (Cambridge, 1972).

[65] David Felix, 'Profit Inflation and Industrial Growth: The Historic Record and Contemporary Analogies', *Quarterly Journal of Economics*, lxx (1956).

[66] William Felkin, *History of the Machine Wrought Hosiery and Lace Manufactures* (Nottingham, 1967).

[67] F. W. Fetter, *The Development of British Monetary Orthodoxy 1797–1875* (Cambridge, Mass., 1965).

[68]   T. W. Fletcher, 'The Great Depression in English Agriculture 1873–1896', *E.H.R.*, 2nd ser., XIII (1961).

[69]   Roderick Floud, 'Changes in the Productivity of Labour in the British Machine-Tool Industry 1856–1900', in *Essays on a Mature Economy: Britain after 1840*, ed. D. N. McCloskey (1972).

[70]   A. G. Ford, 'Overseas Lending and Internal Fluctuations 1870–1914', *Yorkshire Bulletin of Economic and Social Research*, XVII, 1 (1965).

[71]   A. D. Gayer, W. W. Rostow and Anna Schwartz, *The Growth and Fluctuations of the British Economy 1790–1850*, vol. I (Oxford, 1953).

[72]   R. Giffen, *Essays in Finance*, 2nd ed. (1880).

[73]   ——, *Economic Inquiries and Studies*, vol. I (1904).

[74]   O. N. Greeves, 'The Effects of the American Civil War on the Linen and Wool Textile Industries of the U.K.' (unpublished Ph.D. thesis, University of Bristol, 1968–9).

[75]   Pauline Gregg, *A Social and Economic History of Britain 1760–1972*, 7th rev. ed. (1972).

[76]   H. J. Habakkuk, 'Fluctuations and Growth in the 19th Century', in *Studies in Economics and Economic History*, ed. M. Kooy (1972).

[77]   A. R. Hall, *The Export of Capital from Britain 1870–1914* (1968).

[78]   E. J. Hamilton, 'Profit Inflation and the Industrial Revoultion 1750–1800', *Quarterly Journal of Economics*, LVI, 2 (1942).

[79]   John Hicks, *A Theory of Economic History* (Oxford, 1969).

[80]   R. P. Higonnet, 'Bank Deposit in the U.K., 1870–1914', *Quarterly Journal of Economics*, LXXI (1957).

[81]   E. J. Hobsbawm, *Industry and Empire* (1968).

[82]   W. Hoffman, *British Industry 1700–1950* (Oxford, 1955).

[83]   B. A. Holderness, 'Landlords' Capital Formation in East Anglia 1750–1870', *E.H.R.*, 2nd ser., XXV (1972).

[84]   B. C. Hunt, *The Development of the Business Corporation in Britain, 1800–1867* (Cambridge, Mass., 1936).

[85]   W. Isard, 'A Neglected Cycle: The Transport Building Cycle', *Review of Economic Statistics*, XXIV (1942).

[86]   W. L. Jenks, *The Migration of Capital to 1875*, 2nd ed. (1963).

[87]   W. S. Jevons, 'The Depreciation of Gold', in *Investigations in Currency and Finance*, ed. H. S. Foxsell (1909).

[88]   ——, 'On the Variations of Prices and the Value of Currency since 1782', *Journal of the Royal Statistical Society*, XXVIII (1965), and in *Essays in Economic History*, ed. E. M. Carus Wilson, vol. III (1962).

[89] E. L. Jones, 'The Changing Basis of English Agricultural Prosperity 1853–1873', *Agricultural History Review* (1962).

[90] ——, 'The Agricultural Labour Market 1793–1872', *E.H.R.*, 2nd ser., XVII (1964).

[91] Gareth Stedman Jones, *Outcast London* (Oxford, 1971).

[92] J. R. Kellett, *The Impact of Railways on Victorian Cities* (1969).

[93] John Kelly, 'The End of the Famine: The Manchester Cotton Trade, 1864–7', in *Textile History and Economic History*, ed. N. B. Harte and K. G. Ponting (Manchester, 1974).

[94] John Killick, 'Risk, Specialization and Profit in the Mercantile Sector of the Nineteenth-Century Cotton Trade', *Business History*, XVI (1974).

[95] C. P. Kindleberger, 'Foreign Trade and Economic Growth: Lessons From Britain and France, 1850–1913', *E.H.R.*, 2nd ser., XIV (1961).

[96] ——, *Economic Growth in France and Britain 1851–1950* (Cambridge, Mass., 1964).

[97] W. T. C. King, *History of the London Discount Market* (1936).

[98] G. Kitson Clark, *The Making of Victorian England* (1962).

[99] Simon Kuznets, *Secular Movements in Production and Prices* (Boston, 1930).

[100] J. E. Lander, 'Operations in the London Money Market 1858–1867' (unpublished Ph.D. thesis, University of London, 1972).

[101] Leone Levi, *Wages and Earnings of the Working Classes* (1885).

[102] M. Levy-Leboyer, 'La Croissance économique en France au XIXe siècle', *Annales*, XXIII (1968).

[103] A. T. McCabe, 'The Standard of Living on Merseyside 1850–1875', in *Victorian Lancashire*, ed. S. Peter Bell (Newton Abbot, 1974).

[104] Donald McCloskey, 'Did Victorian Britain Fail?', *E.H.R.*, 2nd ser., XXIII (1970).

[105] W. J. Macpherson, 'Investment in Indian Railways 1845–1875', *E.H.R.*, 2nd ser., VIII (1956).

[106] Alfred Marshall, *Industry and Trade* (1919).

[107] Peter Mathias, *The First Industrial Nation* (1969).

[108] R. C. O. Matthews, 'The Trade Cycle in Britain 1790–1850', *Oxford Economic Papers*, VI (1954).

[109] Henry Mayhew, *London Labour and the London Poor* (1851).

[110] John Mills, 'On Credit Cycles and the Origin of Commercial Panics', *Transactions of the Manchester Statistical Society* (1867–8).

[111]   ——, 'On the Post-Panic Period 1866–70', *Transactions of the Manchester Statistical Society* (1870–1).

[112]   B. R. Mitchell and P. Deane, *Abstract of British Historical Statistics* (Cambridge, 1962).

[113]   ——, 'The Coming of the Railways and U.K. Economic Growth', *Journal of Economic History*, xxiv, 3 (1964).

[114]   E. V. Morgan, *The Theory and Practice of Central Banking 1797–1913* (1943).

[115]   J. H. Morris and L. J. Williams, *The South Wales Coal Industry 1841–1875* (Cardiff, 1958).

[116]   A. E. Musson, *Enterprise in Soap and Chemicals: Joseph Crosfield and Sons Ltd., 1815–1965* (Manchester, 1965).

[117]   R. H. Patterson, *The New Golden Age* (1865).

[118]   P. L. Payne, *Rubber and Railways in the Nineteenth Century* (Liverpool, 1961).

[119]   Harold Perkin, *The Origins of Modern English Society 1780–1880* (1969).

[120]   ——, *Inflation, Deflation and Class Conflict Since 1815*; paper read at the International Economic History Association meeting, Leningrad, 1971 (forthcoming).

[121]   F. Perroux, 'Prises de vue sur la croissance de l'économie française 1780–1950', International Association for Research in Income and Wealth, *Income and Wealth*, ser. v (London, 1955).

[122]   E. H. Phelps Brown and S. A. Ozga, 'Economic Growth and the Price Level', *Economic Journal*, lxv (1955).

[123]   —— and B. Weber, 'Accumulation, Productivity and Distribution in the British Economy 1870–1938', in *Essays in Economic History*, ed. E. M. Carus Wilson, vol. iii (1962).

[124]   Sidney Pollard, 'The Decline of Shipbuilding on the Thames, *E.H.R.*, 2nd ser., iii (1950).

[125]   ——, *A History of Labour in Sheffield* (Liverpool, 1959).

[126]   —— and D. W. Crossley, *The Wealth of Britain 1085–1880* (1968).

[127]   Harold Pollins, 'Railway Contractors and the Finance of Railway Development in Britain', *Journal of Transport History*, iii (1957/8).

[128]   J. Potter, 'The Atlantic Economy 1815–1860: the U.S.A. and the Industrial Revolution in Britain', in *Studies in the Industrial Revolution*, ed. L. S. Pressnell (1960).

[129]   John Prest, *The Industrial Revolution in Coventry* (Oxford, 1960).

[130] Arthur Redford, *Manchester Merchants and Foreign Trade*, vol. II (1956).

[131] ——, *The Economic History of England 1750–1860*, 2nd ed. (1960).

[132] H. W. Richardson and J. M. Bass, 'The Profitability of Consett Company before 1914', *Business History*, VII (1965).

[133] W. G. Rimmer, *Marshalls of Leeds, Flax Spinners* (Cambridge, 1960).

[134] M. Rist, 'A French Experiment with Free Trade: The Treaty of 1860', in *Essays in French Economic History*, ed. Rondo Cameron (Illinois, 1970).

[135] Nathan Rosenberg (ed.), *The American System of Manufacturing* (Edinburgh, 1969).

[136] S. B. Saul, *Studies in British Overseas Trade 1870–1914* (Liverpool, 1960).

[137] R. S. Sayers, 'The Question of the Standard in the Eighteen-Fifties', *Economic History*, II (1933).

[138] ——, *Lloyds Bank in the History of English Banking* (Oxford, 1957).

[139] W. Schlote, *British Overseas Trade from 1700 to the 1930s* (Oxford, 1952).

[140] J. A. Schumpeter, *Business Cycles* (New York, 1939).

[141] H. A. Shannon, 'The Limited Companies of 1866–1883', *Economic History*, IV (1933).

[142] Seymour Shapiro, *Capital and the Cotton Industry in the Industrial Revolution* (New York, 1967).

[143] E. M. Sigsworth, 'The West Riding Textile Industries and the Great Exhibition', *Yorkshire Bulletin of Economic and Social Research*, IV (1952).

[144] ——, *Black Dyke Mills: A History* (1958).

[145] Matthew Simon, 'The Pattern of New British Portfolio Foreign Investment 1865–1914', in *Capital Movements and Economic Development*, ed. J. H. Adler (1967).

[146] A. J. Taylor, 'Labour Productivity and Technical Innovation in the British Coal Industry 1850–1914', *E.H.R.*, 2nd ser., XIV, 1 (1961).

[147] Brinley Thomas, *Migration and Economic Growth* (Cambridge, 1973).

[148] F. M. L. Thompson, 'English Great Estates in the 19th Century 1790–1914', First International Conference of Economic History, Stockholm, *Contributions* (1960).

[149] Samuel Timmins (ed.), *The Resources, Products and Industrial History of Birmingham and the Midland Hardware District* (Birmingham, 1866).

[150] Thomas Tooke and W. Newmarch, *History of Prices*, vol. v (1857).

[151] R. E. Tyson, 'The Cotton Industry', in *British Industry and Foreign Competition 1870–1914*, ed. D. H. Aldcroft (1968).

[152] J. Veverka, 'The Growth of Government Expenditure in the U.K. since 1790', *Scottish Journal of Political Economy*, x (1963).

[153] J. E. Wadsworth, 'Banking Ratios Past and Present', in *Essays in Money and Banking*, ed. C. R. Whittlesey and J. S. G. Wilson (Oxford, 1968).

[154] A. A. Walters, *Money in Boom and Slump* (1969).

[155] C. N. Ward-Perkins, 'The Commercial Crisis of 1847', *Oxford Economic Papers*, ii (1950).

[156] John Watts, *The Facts of the Cotton Famine* (1868).

[157] R. K. Webb, *Modern England from the 18th Century to the Present* (1969).

[158] B. Weber, 'A New Index of Residential Construction 1838–1950', *Scottish Journal of Political Economy*, ii (1955).

[159] J. S. G. Williamson, *American Growth and the Balance of Payments 1829–1913* (Chapel Hill, North Carolina, 1964).

[160] G. H. Wood, 'Real Wages and the Standard of Comfort since 1850', *Journal of the Royal Statistical Society*, 72 (1909).

[161] G. H. Wright, *Chronicles of the Commercial Society and Birmingham Chamber of Commerce A.D. 1793–1913* (Birmingham, 1913).

[162] J. F. Wright, 'British Economic Growth 1688–1959', *E.H.R.*, 2nd ser., xviii (1965).

[163] G. M. Young, *Victorian England: Portrait of an Age* (1936).

Index

free trade   59–65

Giffen, Robert   13, 17
glass   14, 48, 50
gold   10, 16–21, 65
Goschen, G. J.   46, 52
Great Depression   9, 11, 37, 39, 51, 58, 72
Great Exhibition, 1851   53
gross national product   23–4, 53

Habakkuk, H. J.   55, 67
Hamilton, E. J.   41
hardware   48–9, 65
Hawke, G. R.   31–4
Hicks, J. R.   37
hides   13, 42, 57
Hobsbawm, E. J.   10, 11, 24, 31, 33–4
Hobson, J. A.   68
Hoffman, Walter   22–3
hosiery   42, 48
Hughes, J. R. T.   19, 21, 43, 46, 47, 49, 55

Imlah, A.   59, 63
imports   57–8, 60–4
income   21
India   28, 59, 65, 68
industrial production   23, 37
innovation   43, 45, 50, 55, 73
interchangeable parts   48
interest, rate of   18, 20–1, 54, 69
iron and steel   14, 31, 42, 43, 45, 49, 50, 57, 59
Isard, W.   35

Jevons, W. S.   13, 16, 17
joint-stock limited liability   54

Keynes, J. M.   40
Kindleberger, C. P.   11
Kondratieff, N. D.   10
Kuznets, S.   10

Landes, D. S.   14, 16, 19
lace   48

Layton, W., and Crowther, G.   10, 14
leather   22, 42, 50
Levi, L.   59
Lewis, J. Parry   36
linen   42
liquidity   18–20
London   35–6, 73

McCloskey, D.   74
Manchester   36
Marshall, A.   49
Mathias, Peter   59, 63
Merseyside   73
Middlesbrough   35, 50
Midlands, see East Midlands
migration   35
Mitchell, B. R.   31, 34
money   16
Morgan, E. V.   11

national income   33, 37–8
Newmarch, W.   16, 17, 21, 33, 74
Nishimura, S.   19

Opium War   64

paper   42, 50
Patterson, R. H.   19
Phelps Brown, E. H.   51, 71
population   35, 74
prices   13–22, 28–9, 41–5, 50, 60
productivity   38, 47, 48
profit   40–2, 44, 50–1, 53–4
protection   60, 62
Prussia   61
public expenditure   26

railway investment   32–3, 68–9, 74
railways   30–4
raw materials   22–3, 52, 60, 64
Redford, A.   53
Rostow, W. W.   10, 14, 20–2; Rostow Paradox   18
Rousseaux, Paul   14